Dear Friends,

I'm your English Buddy!
Forget about all your worries.
I'm here to help you!
Let's smile! Let's learn! And let's have fun!

All the best,
Your English Buddy

★ HOW TO USE ★

재미있는 만화를 통해, 본문에서 배우게 될 내용과 문법을 확인해 보세요!

STORY

과학, 문화, 역사 등 다양한 주제에 대한 재미있고 정보성 가득한 이야기들이 수록되어 있습니다. 앞에서 배운 단어와 문법이 어떻게 쓰였는지 확인하며 독해 실력과 배경지식을 쌓아보세요!

Words to Learn

본격적으로 이야기를 읽기 전에 이야기에 나올 단어를 사진이나 그림과 함께 미리 학습해 보세요!

Grammar to Learn

해당 Unit에서 배울 핵심 문법을 그림과 예시 문장으로 제시했습니다. 독해 실력에 기본이 되는 문법 실력을 한층 더 업그레이드 해 보세요!

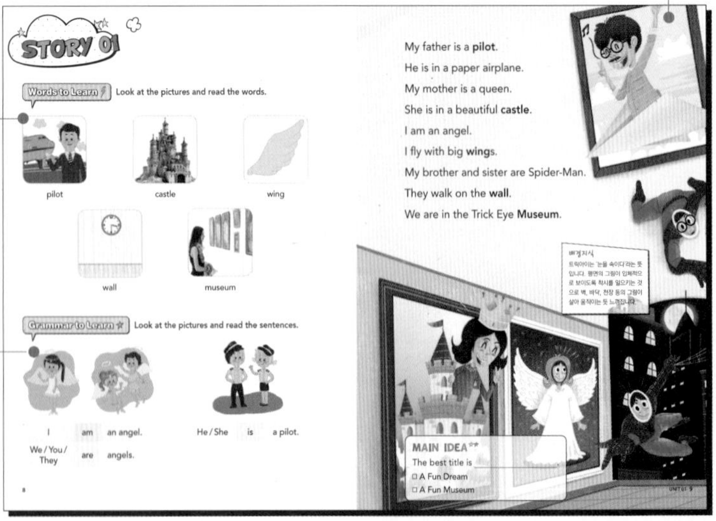

Word Check

앞서 배운 단어를 문제를 통해 확인해 볼 차례입니다. 그림 및 사진과 맞는 단어를 찾아보며 단어 실력을 점검해 보세요!

Grammar Check

간단한 문법 문제를 통해 이야기에 등장한 주요 문법을 제대로 학습했는지 점검해 보세요!

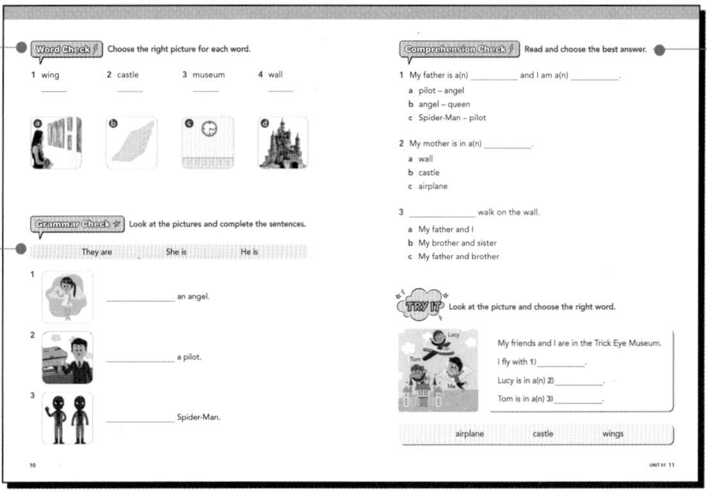

Word Check Choose the right picture for each word.

1 wing 2 castle 3 museum 4 wall

Grammar Check Look at the pictures and complete the sentences.

They are / She is / He is

1 ________ an angel.

2 ________ a pilot.

3 ________ Spider-Man.

Comprehension Check Read and choose the best answer.

1 My father is a(n) ________ and I am a(n) ________.
a pilot – angel
b angel – queen
c Spider-Man – pilot

2 My mother is in a(n) ________.
a wall
b castle
c airplane

3 ________ walk on the wall.
a My father and I
b My brother and sister
c My father and brother

TRY IT Look at the picture and choose the right word.

My friends and I are in the Trick Eye Museum.
I fly with 1) ________.
Lucy is in a(n) 2) ________.
Tom is in a(n) 3) ________.

airplane castle wings

10 UNIT 01 11

Comprehension Check

이야기를 잘 이해했는지 확인할 수 있는 문제들이 실려 있습니다. TRY IT 코너에서 조금 더 어려운 문제에도 도전하며 실력을 강화해 보세요!

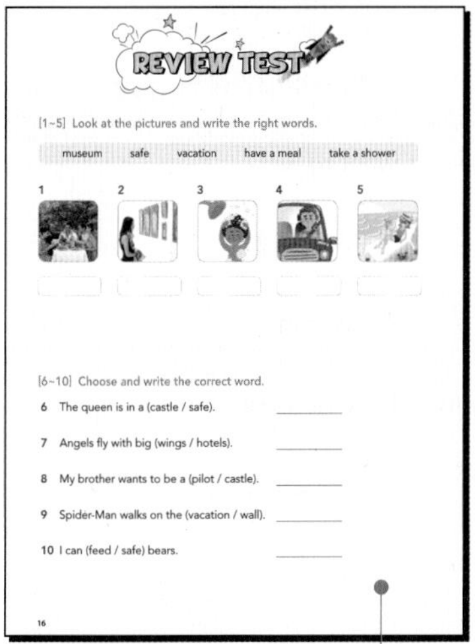

REVIEW TEST

[1~5] Look at the pictures and write the right words.

museum safe vacation have a meal take a shower

1 2 3 4 5

[6~10] Choose and write the correct word.

6 The queen is in a (castle / safe).

7 Angels fly with big (wings / hotels).

8 My brother wants to be a (pilot / castle).

9 Spider-Man walks on the (vacation / wall).

10 I can (feed / safe) bears.

16

재미있는 쉬어가기 코너를 통해 학습으로 지친 머리를 식혀보세요!

REVIEW TEST

각 Unit에서 학습한 단어와 문법, 그리고 이야기에 대한 이해도를 확인할 수 있는 다양한 문제가 실려 있습니다. 앞서 배운 내용을 다시 한번 확인해 보세요!

WORKBOOK

각 Unit에서 배운 단어와 문법을 여러 문제를 통해 확인하고 정리해 보세요.

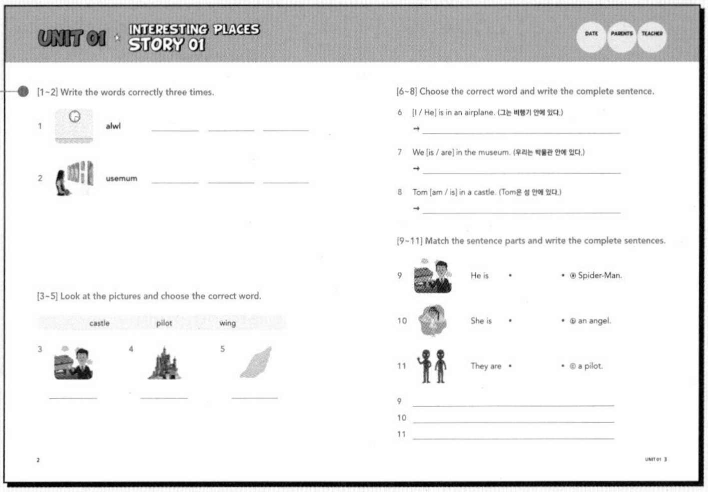

UNIT 01 INTERESTING PLACES STORY 01

DATE PARENTS TEACHER

[1~2] Write the words correctly three times.

1 alwl

2 usemum

[3~5] Look at the pictures and choose the correct word.

castle pilot wing

3 4 5

[6~8] Choose the correct word and write the complete sentence.

6 [I / He] is in an airplane. (그는 비행기 안에 있다.)

7 We [is / are] in the museum. (우리는 박물관 안에 있다.)

8 Tom [am / is] in a castle. (Tom은 성 안에 있다.)

[9~11] Match the sentence parts and write the complete sentences.

9 He is • • ⓐ Spider-Man.

10 She is • • ⓑ an angel.

11 They are • • ⓒ a pilot.

2 UNIT 01 3

☆ OVERVIEW OF READING BUDDY ☆

	Unit	Title	Story	Key Words	Key Grammar
Level 1	01	INTERESTING PLACES	1	pilot, castle, wing, wall, museum	인칭대명사와 be동사
			2	vacation, hotel, have a meal, take a shower, feed, safe	명사의 복수형
	02	HEALTH	1	itchy, peanut, dangerous, see a doctor, take medicine	일반동사 현재형의 부정문
			2	gain weight, plate, taste, exercise, forget, hunger	명령문
	03	SPECIAL JOBS	1	perfect, lie down, leave, miss, chance	조동사 can
			2	pet, strange, worried, chew, swallow	be동사의 의문문
	04	HOBBIES	1	skate, jump, pass, fall down, hurt	일반동사의 3인칭 단수형
			2	collect, famous, touch, locked, unlock	want to-v
	05	NATURE	1	scared, hide, protect, bring, each other	형용사의 역할
			2	shine, sunny, sticky, get away, weak	조동사 can't
	06	SCHOOL LIFE	1	sweep, wipe, empty, trash can, erase, plant	It's time to-v
			2	get up, wash, get dressed, have breakfast, favorite	일반동사의 의문문
	07	SAVE THE EARTH	1	action, save the Earth, bottle, waste, recycle	청유문
			2	polar bear, the North Pole, spend, visit, tour, break	부정명령문
	08	FAIRY TALES	1	be lost, woods, cold, yummy, bread	There is/are
			2	magic, lamp, wish, comic book, cozy	Here is/are
Level 2	01	FOOD & COOKING	1	follow, recipe, cucumber, carrot, add	일반동사의 과거형
			2	astronaut, vegetable, hard, package, pour, microwave	의문사
	02	SPECIAL DAYS	1	the United States, celebrate, chocolate, interesting, each other	시간을 나타내는 전치사
			2	pick up, several, choose, athlete, rich	관사 the
	03	SUPERHEROES	1	prison, peace, delivery, fast, climb	조동사 will
			2	cape, resemble, attack, be afraid of, strong, train	등위접속사 and, but
	04	MY PET	1	apartment, bark, loudly, neighbor, allergic	셀 수 있는 명사와 셀 수 없는 명사
			2	grow, smart, smile, greet, guest	형용사의 순서

	Unit	Title	Story	Key Words	Key Grammar
	05	CULTURE	1	first, sour, second, beak, third	call+목적어+목적보어
			2	invite, dessert, tooth, hold, coin, tradition	What으로 시작하는 감탄문
	06	GOOD LUCK & BAD LUCK	1	symbol, around the world, wave, bill, wallet	장소를 나타내는 전치사
			2	mirror, broken, fence, sign, fail one's test	위치를 나타내는 전치사
	07	TRAVEL THE WORLD	1	travel, careful, rule, subway, flush the toilet, pay a fine	조동사 should
			2	be made of, worry, sleeping bag, fun, afternoon	go+v-ing
	08	HOW STRANGE!	1	win, try one's best, terrible, wear, playground, step	일반동사 과거형의 부정문
			2	stick, behavior, colorful, cover, start	how+형용사 ~?
Level 3	01	MONEY	1	clerk, stone, thankfully, carry, owner	원급 비교
			2	save, piggy bank, piglet, grow, sick	비교급
	02	ENVIRONMENT	1	climb, heavy, oxygen bottle, among, light, trash	최상급
			2	scientist, cow, hurt, fart, burp	감탄문
	03	MY OPINION	1	hallway, enter, behave, record, uncomfortable	감각동사+형용사
			2	learn, draw, outside, lake, nature, miss	빈도부사
	04	SHOPPING	1	cart, way, reason, full, push, secret	목적보어가 있는 동사
			2	look for, flavor, price, be made from, cheaply, fair	종속접속사 when, because, if
	05	GOOD INVENTIONS	1	normal, press, remote control, pick up, technology, convenient	감각동사+형용사 vs. 감각동사 like+명사
			2	across, invent, traffic light, side, copy	동명사 vs. to부정사
	06	TECHNOLOGY	1	sign, painting, rule, visitor, blind	조동사 may
			2	turn off, connect, machine, control, break down	현재진행형
	07	IN SPACE	1	astronaut, space, float, spaceship, tie	조동사 must, have to
			2	turn on, shoot, loud, silent, turn down	조동사 must와 cannot
	08	TRADITIONS	1	doll, worry, take away, pillow, disappear	tell+간접목적어+직접목적어
			2	hang from, cliff, hold onto, honey, hive, fall	동명사의 역할

CONTENTS

UNIT 01
INTERESTING PLACES
Read and guess the stories.
They are Spider-Man.
He is a pilot.
You can have a meal with lions.

STORY 01

Words to Learn

Look at the pictures and read the words.

pilot

castle

wing

wall

museum

Grammar to Learn

Look at the pictures and read the sentences.

I	am	an angel.
We / You / They	are	angels.

He / She	is	a pilot.

My father is a **pilot**.

He is in a paper airplane.

My mother is a queen.

She is in a beautiful **castle**.

I am an angel.

I fly with big **wing**s.

My brother and sister are Spider-Man.

They walk on the **wall**.

We are in the Trick Eye **Museum**.

배경지식

트릭아이는 '눈을 속이다'라는 뜻입니다. 평면의 그림이 입체적으로 보이도록 착시를 일으키는 것으로 벽, 바닥, 천장 등의 그림이 살아 움직이는 듯 느껴집니다.

MAIN IDEA ☆☆

The best title is ________________.

□ A Fun Dream

□ A Fun Museum

Word Check Choose the right picture for each word.

1 wing ______

2 castle ______

3 museum ______

4 wall ______

a 

b 

c 

d 

Grammar Check Look at the pictures and complete the sentences.

They are | She is | He is

1 

______ an angel.

2 

______ a pilot.

3 

______ Spider-Man.

Comprehension Check

Read and choose the best answer.

1 My father is a(n) __________ and I am a(n) __________.

a pilot – angel

b angel – queen

c Spider-Man – pilot

2 My mother is in a(n) __________.

a wall

b castle

c airplane

3 ______________ walk on the wall.

a My father and I

b My brother and sister

c My father and brother

TRY IT

Look at the picture and choose the right word.

My friends and I are in the Trick Eye Museum.

I fly with **1)** __________.

Lucy is in a(n) **2)** __________.

Tom is in a(n) **3)** __________.

airplane	castle	wings

STORY 02

Words to Learn

Look at the pictures and read the words.

vacation

hotel

have a meal

take a shower

feed

safe

Grammar to Learn

Look at the pictures and read the words.

a lion	three **lions**
a bear	two **bears**

a shark	two **sharks**
a sheep	two **sheep**

Do you want to have a special **vacation**?

Do you like animals?

Then come to our zoo **hotel**.

You can **have a meal** with lions.

You can **take a shower** with bears.

You can sleep with sharks.

You can **feed** giraffes in your room.

But don't worry. It is **safe**.

MAIN IDEA ☆☆

The best title is ____________________.

☐ Dangerous Animals

☐ An Interesting Hotel

Word Check Match the words to the pictures.

1 vacation 2 feed 3 safe 4 have a meal

Grammar Check Look at the pictures and correct the underlined words.

1 

You can take a shower with a giraffe. ______________

2 

You can feed a lion in your room. ______________

3 

You can have a meal with a shark. ______________

Comprehension Check
Read and choose the best answer.

1 In this hotel, there are lions, bears, ______________.

a sharks, and sheep
b sharks, and giraffes
c penguins, and rabbits

2 You can take a shower with __________.

a lions
b bears
c sharks

3 You can __________ with sharks.

a feed
b sleep
c take a shower

TRY IT
Read and choose the right words.

Visit the zoo hotel!

You can 1) ______________ with lions.

You can 2) ______________ with bears.

You can 3) ______________ giraffes.

feed   have a meal   take a shower

REVIEW TEST

[1~5] Look at the pictures and write the right words.

museum   safe   vacation   have a meal   take a shower

1

2

3

4

5

[6~10] Choose and write the correct word.

6 The queen is in a (castle / safe). ____________

7 Angels fly with big (wings / hotels). ____________

8 My brother wants to be a (pilot / castle). ____________

9 Spider-Man walks on the (vacation / wall). ____________

10 I can (feed / safe) bears. ____________

[11~12] Look at the pictures and choose the right words.

11 am are is

We __________ in the museum.

12 giraffes a giraffe a giraffes

You can feed __________.

[13~14] Read and answer.

Do you want to have a special vacation?
Do you like animals?
Then come to our zoo hotel.
You can have a meal with lions.
You can take a shower with bears.
You can sleep with sharks.
You can feed giraffes in your room.
But don't worry. It is __________.

13 Check True or False.

a You can take a shower with bears. True False

b You can feed sharks in your room. True False

14 Choose the word for the blank.

a safe

b scary

c dangerous

당신은 어떤 색 풍선을 선물할 건가요?

공원을 지나가다 마음에 드는 이성 발견! 어떤 색 풍선으로 이성의 마음을 사로잡을 건가요?
빨간 풍선, 노란 풍선, 파란 풍선, 하얀 풍선 중 골라 보세요!
그러면, 내가 어떤 성격을 가진 사람인지 알 수 있을 거예요!

빨간 풍선을 선택한 당신!

겉으로는 밝고 활발하지만
속은 상처가 많은 타입이군요.

노란 풍선을 선택한 당신!

순수하고 솔직한 타입입니다.
너무 사람을 잘 믿어 이용을
당할 수 있으니 조심하는 게 좋아요!

파란 풍선을 선택한 당신!

마음에 드는 상대가 나타나면
적극적으로 다가가는 당신,
성격이 좋고 대인관계가 좋아
인기가 많네요.

하얀 풍선을 선택한 당신!

솔직하지 못한 타입으로
누구에게나 마음을 털어놓기
힘들어하고, 수줍음이 많군요.

UNIT 02
HEALTH
Read and guess the stories.
I don't eat peanuts. I have an allergy.
Put your food on a blue plate. It doesn't look delicious.

STORY 01

Words to Learn

Look at the pictures and read the words.

itchy

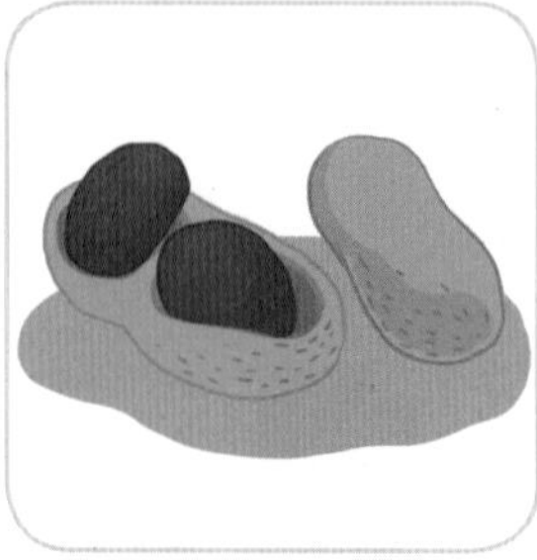

peanut

dangerous

see a doctor

take medicine

Grammar to Learn

Look at the pictures and read the sentences.

I / You / We	**don't eat**	peaches.

He / She	**doesn't eat**	shrimps.
They	**don't eat**	

Bill doesn't eat peaches.

His fingers become **itchy**.

His sister doesn't eat shrimps.

Her lips become big.

His twin brothers don't eat **peanuts**.

Their cheeks become red.

These are allergies!

They can be **dangerous**.

See a doctor quickly

and **take medicine**.

배경지식

음식물 알레르기란 해롭지 않은 음식물임에도 먹으면 몸이 과잉 반응을 나타내는 것을 말합니다. 다양한 증상이 있으나, 몸의 일부가 붓거나 가려운 경우가 많습니다. 흔히 알레르기를 일으키는 음식으로는 땅콩이나 호두 같은 견과류, 조개, 새우, 게 등의 해산물, 그리고 복숭아, 키위 등의 과일이 있습니다.

MAIN IDEA ☆★

The best title is ____________.

☐ Delicious Food

☐ Dangerous Allergies

Word Check Match the words to the pictures.

1 peanut

2 itchy

3 dangerous

4 take medicine

a
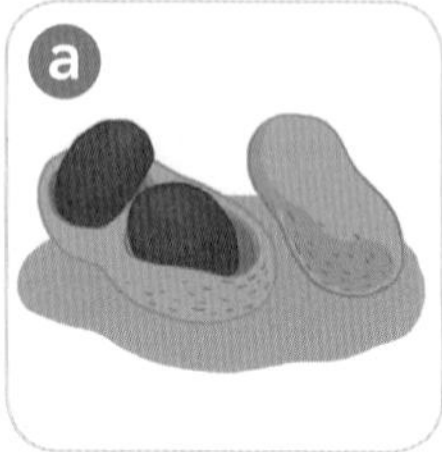

b

c

d

Grammar Check Circle the correct word for each sentence.

1 I (don't / doesn't) eat shrimps.

2 He (don't / doesn't) have allergies.

3 You (don't / doesn't) eat peaches.

4 They (don't / doesn't) take medicine.

5 James (don't / doesn't) see a doctor.

Comprehension Check

Read and choose the best answer.

1 Peaches make Bill's ________ itchy.

a lips
b cheeks
c fingers

2 Bill's sister has allergy to ________.

a shrimps
b peanuts
c peaches

3 Allergies can be ________.

a safe
b funny
c dangerous

TRY IT

Read and fill in the blanks.

Food		Allergies
	➡	Bill's fingers become **1)** ________.
	➡	Bill's sister's lips become **2)** ________.
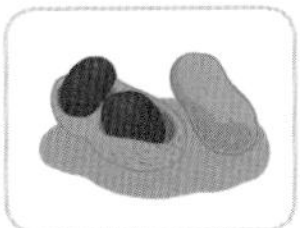	➡	Bill's brothers' cheeks become **3)** ________.

STORY 02

Words to Learn

Look at the pictures and read the words.

gain weight

plate

taste

exercise

forget

hunger

Grammar to Learn

Look at the picture and read the sentences.

Eat	less.
Do	some exercises.
Ride	a bicycle.

I love eating.

Everything is delicious to me.

But I don't want to **gain weight**.

How can I eat less?

↳ Put your food on a blue **plate**.

It doesn't look delicious.

↳ Brush your teeth.

The food doesn't **taste** good.

↳ Do some **exercises**.

You can **forget** your **hunger**.

Think!

I don't want to gain weight.

What can I do?

1. ______________________

2. ______________________

MAIN IDEA ☆☆

This story is about ______________.

☐ eating less

☐ cooking well

Word Check Choose the right picture for each word.

1 plate ______ 2 taste ______ 3 exercise ______ 4 forget ______

Grammar Check Look at the pictures and complete the sentences.

do brush put

1 

______ your teeth.

2 

______ some exercises.

3 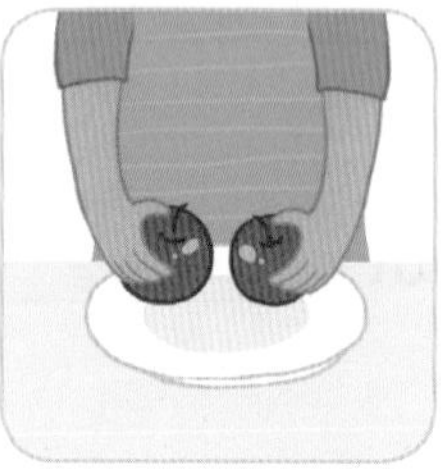

______ the apples on a plate.

Comprehension Check

Read and choose the best answer.

1 The girl wants to ______________.

a eat less

b cook well

c gain weight

2 Your food doesn't look delicious on a __________ plate.

a red

b blue

c yellow

3 __________ can make you forget your hunger.

a Sleep

b Music

c Exercises

TRY IT

Read and choose the right words.

You want to eat less. What can you do?

➡ I can put food on 1) ______________.

➡ I can brush 2) ______________.

➡ I can do 3) ______________.

my teeth	a blue plate	some exercises

REVIEW TEST

[1~5] Look at the pictures and write the right words.

dangerous gain weight peanut take medicine see a doctor

1

2

3

4

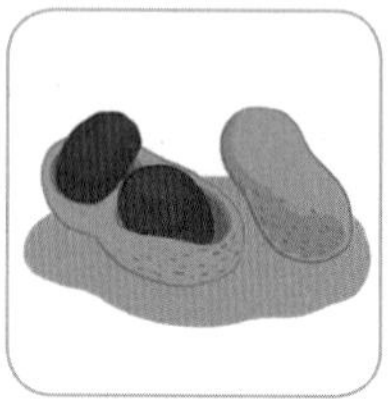

5

[6~10] Choose and write the correct word.

6 They do some (lips / exercises) every day. ____________

7 I put food on a white (cheek / plate). ____________

8 My fingers become (peanut / itchy). ____________

9 The peaches (taste / forget) delicious. ____________

10 I don't want to (forget / itchy) your name. ____________

[11~12] Choose the right words.

11 Do Does Don't

__________ some exercises.

12 eat don't eat doesn't eat

My brother __________ shrimps.

[13~14] Read and answer.

Bill doesn't eat peaches.
His fingers become itchy.

His sister doesn't eat shrimps.
Her lips become big.

His twin brothers don't eat peanuts.
Their cheeks become red.

These are allergies!
They can be dangerous.
See a doctor quickly and take medicine.

13 Check True or False.

a Peaches make Bill's fingers itchy. True False

b Shrimps make Bill's sister's lips red. True False

c Peanuts make Bill's brothers' cheeks big. True False

14 They __________ because they have allergies.

a eat the food

b see a doctor

c drink a lot of water

재미있는 동물 이야기

아무도 몰랐던 동물들의 비밀을 알고 싶다면 아래의 OX퀴즈를 풀어보세요.

Q: 판다의 눈 주위가 검은 것은 눈을 크게 보이게 해서 귀엽게 보이기 위함이다?

O

X

정답은 X

판다의 눈 주위에 있는 검은 털 덕분에 판다가 더 귀여워 보이는 것은 사실이다.
하지만 이것은 미모를 위해서가 아니라 적으로부터 판다 자신을 보호하기 위함이라는 것!
동물들은 보통 눈이 약해서 자주 공격을 당하는데 판다는 적이 눈의 위치를 쉽게 알 수 없어서 눈을 보호할 수 있다!

Q: 북극곰은 검은색 피부를 갖고 있다?

O

X

정답은 O

콜라 마시는 그 귀여운 북극곰의 피부가 검은색이라고?
그렇다. 그렇다면 하얀 털 때문에 북극곰은 하얗게 보이는 것일까?
그렇지 않다. 북극곰의 털은 반투명하다. 그렇다면 왜 우리 눈에는 북극곰이 흰색으로 보일까?
북극곰의 반투명한 털이 햇빛에 반사되어 우리의 눈에 하얗게 보이는 것이다.

SPECIAL JOBS
UNIT 03
Read and guess the stories.
You eat pet food.
Am I strange? It's my job.
Are you tired?
No, it's my job. I can get money because I lie down all day.

STORY 01

Words to Learn Look at the pictures and read the words.

perfect

lie down

leave

miss

chance

Grammar to Learn Look at the pictures and read the sentences.

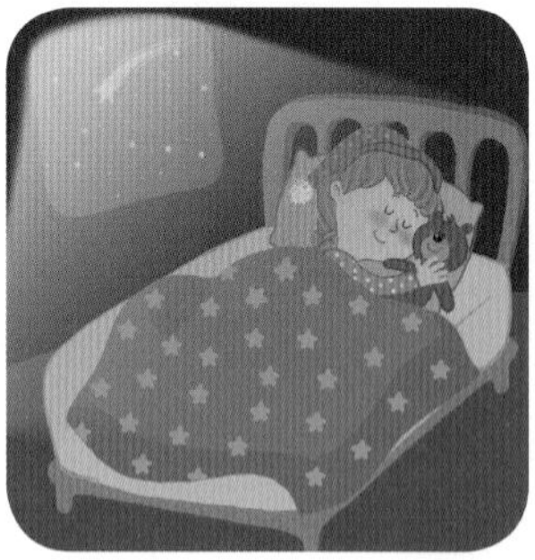

I You She	can	sleep. get money.

We You They	can	lie down. watch TV.

Do you like lying in bed?

This job is **perfect** for you.

Just **lie down** in bed all day.

You can sleep 8 hours.

You can play games.

You can watch TV.

But you can't **leave** the bed.

You can get 5,000 dollars a month.

Don't **miss** this **chance**.

배경지식

실제로 NASA(미국항공우주국)에서는 이렇게 하루 종일 누워 있을 사람을 구하고 있습니다. 이 일을 통해 우주비행사가 우주에 오래 있으면, 뼈와 근육이 어떻게 변하는지 알아본답니다.

MAIN IDEA ☆☆

This story is about ____________.

☐ a job

☐ a bed

Word Check Match the words to the pictures.

1 leave 2 miss 3 lie down 4 perfect

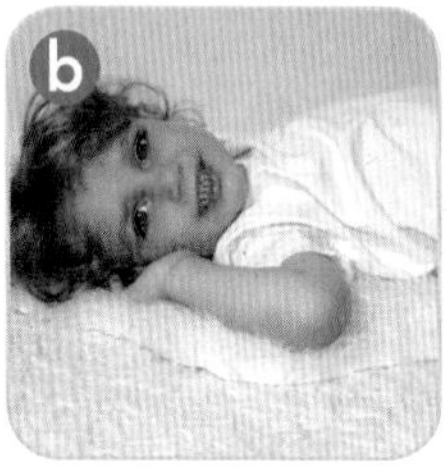

Grammar Check Look at the example and complete the sentences.

You play computer games.
➡ You ___can play___ computer games.

1 He leaves the bed.
➡ He ____________ the bed.

2 They get a lot of money.
➡ They ____________ a lot of money.

Comprehension Check Read and choose the best answer.

1 For this job, you can ______________ in bed all day.

a sleep
b lie down
c meet people

2 You can get __________ dollars a month.

a 3,000
b 4,000
c 5,000

3 What can't you do?

a 

b 

c 

TRY IT Read and choose the right words.

Your job is lying in bed.

1) You can …	2) You can't …

watch TV
play games
leave the bed
sleep 8 hours

STORY 02

Words to Learn

Look at the pictures and read the words.

pet

strange

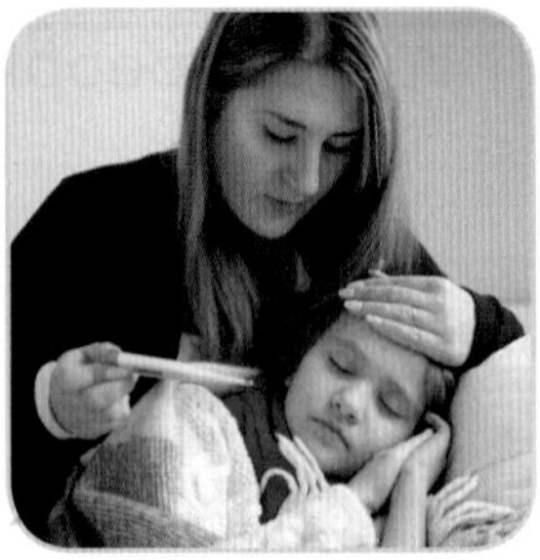

worried

chew

swallow

Grammar to Learn ☆

Look at the pictures and read the sentences.

Am I	strange?
Are you	pretty?

Is she / he	worried?
Are we / they	happy?

I eat **pet** food.

Am I **strange**?

Well, it is my job.

Pets eat special food.

But like us, pets enjoy delicious food.

I taste their food.

I find the delicious food.

Are you **worried** about my health?

Don't worry. I only **chew** the food.

I don't **swallow** it.

MAIN IDEA

The best title is ________________.

□ My Special Job

□ My Special Pet

Word Check

Choose the right picture for each word.

1 pet ________

2 swallow ________

3 worried ________

4 chew ________

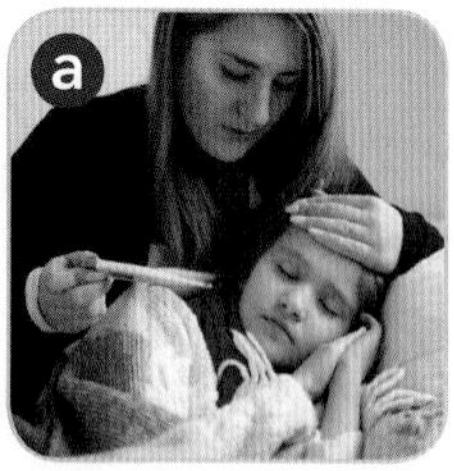

Grammar Check

Look at the example and change the sentences.

You are worried.

➡ Are you worried?

1 They are happy.

➡ ______________________

2 He is strange.

➡ ______________________

3 I am lazy.

➡ ______________________

Comprehension Check

Read and choose the best answer.

1 Pets like __________ food.

a hot
b fresh
c delicious

2 The man __________ delicious food for pets.

a buys
b finds
c cooks

3 The man chews the pet food, but he doesn't __________ it.

a enjoy
b taste
c swallow

TRY IT

Read and choose the right words.

My Job

I am a pet food tester.

I **1)** ______________ pet food.

I find **2)** ______________ for pets.

Don't **3)** ______________ my health, because I don't swallow the food.

taste	worry about	delicious food

REVIEW TEST

[1~5] Look at the pictures and write the right words.

leave	lie down	strange	chance	pet

1

2

3

4

5

[6~10] Choose and write the correct word.

6 This job is (perfect / worried) for you. __________

7 Don't (eat / miss) this chance. __________

8 I am (strange / worried) about my health. __________

9 Dogs (chew / miss) the food. __________

10 I don't (swallow / lie down) the pet food. __________

[11~12] Look at the pictures and correct the underlined parts.

11 You can't watch TV.

→ You ___________ watch TV.

12 She is worried about the test?

→ ________________ about the test?

[13~14] Read and answer.

I eat pet food.
Am I strange?
Well, it is my job.
Pets eat special food.
But like us, pets enjoy delicious food.
I taste their food.
I find the delicious food.
Are you worried about my health?
Don't worry. I only chew the food.
I don't swallow it.

13 The man's job is ________________.

a selling pet food

b tasting pet food

c cooking pet food

14 Check True or False.

a	Pets eat special pet food.	True	False
b	The man is worried about his health.	True	False
c	The man swallows the pet food.	True	False

세계 각지의 독특한 인사법

'티벳'
메롱하듯이 혀를 내밀면서 인사해요.
친근감의 표현이라고 해요.

'이누이트족'
상대방의 뺨을 때리며 인사해요.
반가움의 표현이라고 해요.

'미얀마'
팔짱을 낀 상태로 고개를 숙여 인사를 해요.
팔짱을 끼는 것이 상대방을 존중한다는
의미라고 하네요.

UNIT 04
HOBBIES
Read and guess the stories.
He skates very well. I want to skate well, too.
My dad loves toys. He has 300 toys!
Wow, I want to play with them!

STORY 01

Words to Learn Look at the pictures and read the words.

skate

jump

pass

fall down

hurt

Grammar to Learn Look at the pictures and read the sentences.

	like	skating.
I	**have**	in-line skates.
	go	skating every day.

	likes	skating.
He	**has**	in-line skates.
	goes	skating every day.

Amy loves in-line skating.

She **skate**s very well.

She goes very far.

She **jump**s very high.

She **pass**es everyone very quickly.

CRASH!

She **fall**s **down**.

She **hurt**s her arm.

She goes to the hospital.

She says goodbye to her in-line skates.

MAIN IDEA ☆☆

The best title is ________________.

☐ Amy and Her Bike

☐ Amy and Her In-line Skates

Word Check Match the words to the pictures.

1 jump 2 fall down 3 pass 4 skate

Grammar Check Circle the correct word for each sentence.

1 Amy (run / runs) far.

2 I (skate / skates) very well.

3 She (go / goes) to the bookstore.

4 He (pass / passes) everyone quickly.

5 They (say / says) goodbye to their friends.

Comprehension Check Read and choose the best answer.

1 Amy __________ very high.

a runs

b jumps

c passes

2 Amy goes to the hospital, because ______________.

a she falls down

b she skates well

c she jumps high

3 Amy hurts her __________.

a leg

b arm

c head

TRY IT Number the sentences in the correct order.

	1	Amy skates very fast.
1)	______	Amy goes to the hospital.
2)	______	Amy hurts her arm.
3)	______	Amy falls down.
4)	______	Amy says goodbye to her in-line skates.

STORY 02

Words to Learn

Look at the pictures and read the words.

collect

famous

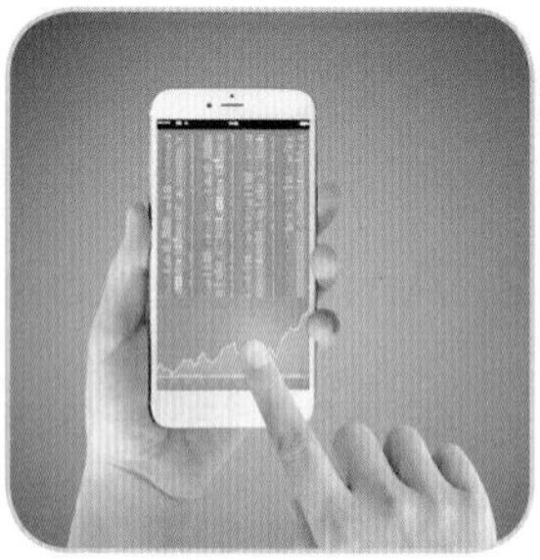

touch

locked

unlock

Grammar to Learn

Look at the pictures and read the sentences.

I want to have dolls.
I want to play with them.

He wants to have toys.
He wants to put toys in his cabinet.

My father is 41 years old.

But he still wants to have toys.

He **collects** them in his cabinet.

They are **famous** superheroes and robots.

They are cool. I want to play with them.

But I can't **touch** them.

The cabinet is always **locked**.

Dad, please **unlock** the cabinet!

배경지식

키덜트는 어린이를 뜻하는 '키즈(kids)'와 성인을 뜻하는 '어덜트(adult)'의 합성어로 어린이와 같은 감성과 취향을 지닌 어른을 의미합니다.

MAIN IDEA ☆☆

The best title is ______________.

□ My Father Likes Toys

□ My Father Likes Movies

Word Check Choose the right picture for each word.

1 locked ______ 2 famous ______ 3 touch ______ 4 collect ______

a

b

c

d

Grammar Check Look at the example and complete the sentences.

I collect superheroes.
➡ I __want to collect__ superheroes.

1 He unlocks the cabinet.
➡ He ________________ the cabinet.

2 I play with robots.
➡ I ________________ with robots.

3 She has many bags.
➡ She ________________ many bags.

Comprehension Check — Read and choose the best answer.

1 The boy's father loves __________ toys.

a cleaning

b collecting

c playing with

2 The boy's father puts the toys in his __________.

a car

b box

c cabinet

3 What are his father's toys?

a 

b 

c 

TRY IT — Read and choose the right word.

My Diary

My father 1) __________ toys in his cabinet.

I want to 2) __________ with them, but I can't.

The cabinet is 3) __________.

play
collects
locked

REVIEW TEST

[1~5] Look at the pictures and write the right words.

fall down　　skate　　unlock　　locked　　touch

1

2

3

4

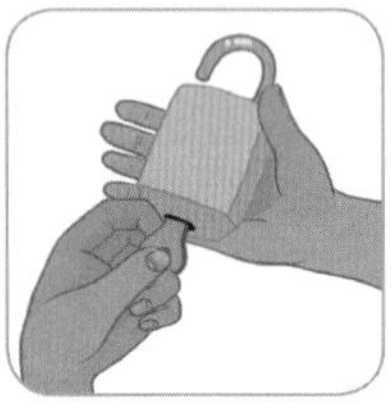

5

[6~10] Choose and write the correct word.

6 Tom (jumps / unlocks) very high. ____________

7 Amy (hurts / collects) toys. ____________

8 They are (high / famous) superheroes. ____________

9 I (pass / skate) everyone quickly. ____________

10 My father (hurts / falls down) his arm. ____________

[11~12] Read and choose the correct words.

11 go gos goes

She ____________ to the hospital.

12 want want to wants to

I ____________ play computer games.

[13~14] Read and answer.

My father is 41 years old.
But he still wants to have toys.
He collects them in his cabinet.
They are famous superheroes and robots.
They are cool. I want to play with them.
But I can't touch them.
The cabinet is always locked.
Dad, please unlock the cabinet!

13 His father's hobby is ________________.

a collecting toys
b playing games
c watching movies

14 Choose True or False.

a The boy's father collects famous robot toys.	True	False
b The boy can play with his father's toys.	True	False
c The cabinet is always unlocked.	True	False

재미있는 착시의 세계

어느 접시의 음식이 더 많아 보이나요?

① ②

다음의 그림들을 보고 크기를 비교해 보세요.

어느 사각형이 더 커 보이나요?

① ②

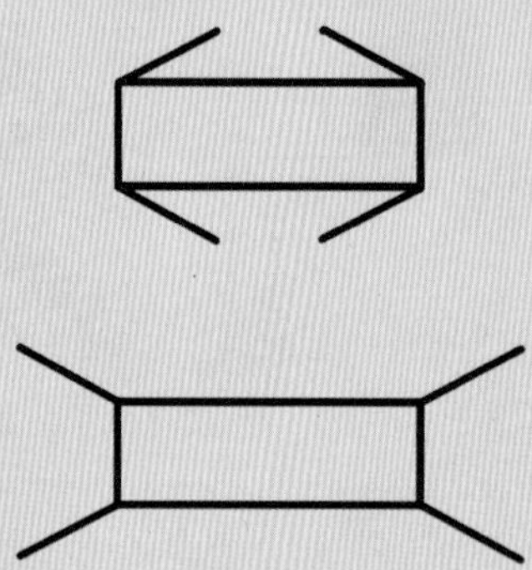

어느 선이 더 길어 보이나요?

① ②

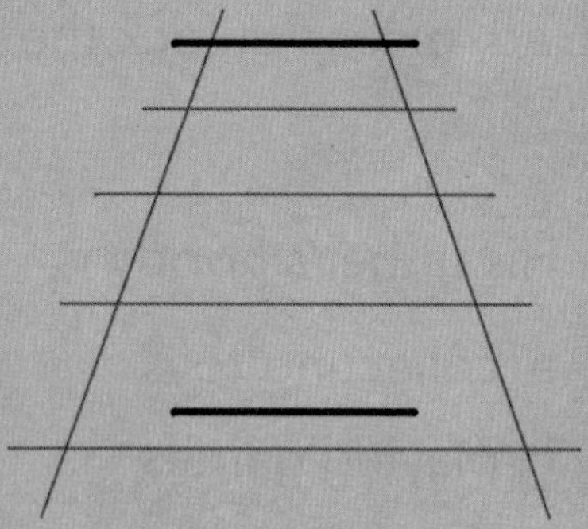

정답은 "모두같다" 입니다.
사실, 접시에 담긴 음식의 양과 사각형의 크기, 선의 길이는 모두 같답니다.
우리의 뇌는 주변의 정보를 바탕으로 크기를 인식하는데, 주변 사물이 얼마나 크고 작은지에 따라 같은 크기의 도형도 서로 크기가 달라 보이는 것입니다.

UNIT 05
NATURE
Read and guess the stories.
I'm a hungry fish!
I'm scared!
My house is sticky. You can't get away.
I'm scared.

STORY 01

Words to Learn Look at the pictures and read the words.

scared

hide

protect

bring

each other

Grammar to Learn Look at the pictures and read the sentences.

He is	**hungry.**
I am	**scared.**

I want	**delicious**	food.
You are a	**good**	friend.

배경지식

서로 다른 두 종이 서로 도움을 주고 받으며 생존하는 것을 공생이라고 합니다. 말미잘과 흰동가리는 공생관계입니다. 말미잘은 흰동가리를 적으로부터 보호해 주고 흰동가리는 옮겨다니지 못하는 말미잘에게 먹이를 가져다 줍니다.

Hey, are you okay?

I am very **scared**.

A hungry fish wants to eat me.

Come here and **hide** in me.

I can **protect** you.

Thank you.

You always help me.

You're welcome! You help me, too.

You **bring** me delicious food.

We help **each other**.

We are good friends.

MAIN IDEA ☆☆

The best title is ______________.

□ Good Food

□ Good Friends

Word Check

Choose the right picture for each word.

1 protect ______

2 hide ______

3 scared ______

4 each other ______

a 

b 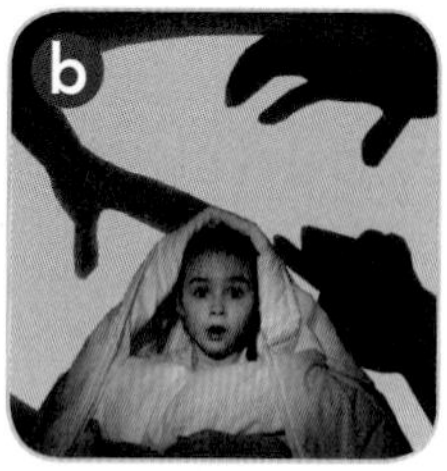

c 

d 

Grammar Check

Look at the pictures and complete the sentences.

scared   hungry   delicious

1 

The boy is ____________.

2 

I can cook ____________ food.

3 

They are very ____________.

Comprehension Check

Read and choose the best answer.

1 The fish is scared because ______________.

a it is hungry

b people want to catch it

c a hungry fish wants to eat it

2 The fish gives its friend __________.

a food

b a fish

c a house

3 They are good friends because ______________.

a they eat together

b they look the same

c they help each other

TRY IT

Read and choose the right word.

You 1) __________ me.

You 2) __________ me food.

We 3) __________ each other.

bring

help

protect

STORY 02

Words to Learn

Look at the pictures and read the words.

shine

sunny

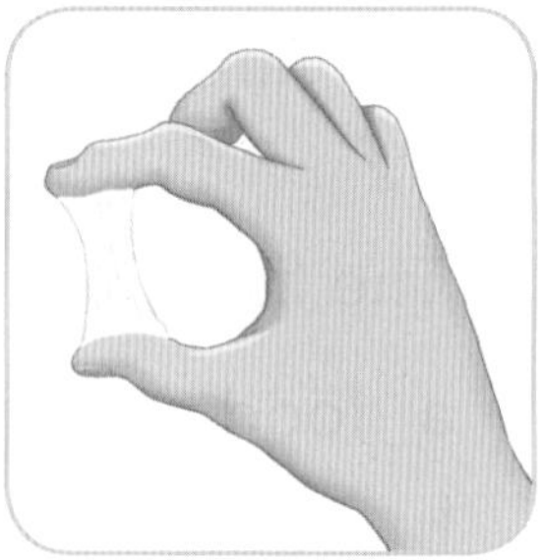

sticky

get away

weak

Grammar to Learn

Look at the pictures and read the sentences.

We **can't** move.
get away.

I **can't** catch them.
eat them.

My house is silver.

It **shine**s on a **sunny** day.

Butterflies and ants can't see it.

My house is **sticky**.

It catches butterflies and ants.

They can't **get away**.

And I eat them.

Rain makes my house **weak**.

Then it can't catch butterflies or ants.

So I become hungry!

배경지식

곤충들은 거미줄에 걸리면 움직일 수 없는데, 거미는 어떻게 자유롭게 움직일 수 있을까요? 그것은 바로 거미줄에는 끈적이는 부분과 아닌 부분이 있기 때문입니다. 거미는 끈적이는 부분을 피해서 자유롭게 움직일 수 있습니다. 또한 거미의 발에서 일종의 기름이 나오기 때문에 다리가 끈적이는 부분에 닿더라도 달라붙지 않습니다.

MAIN IDEA ☆☆

The best title is ______________.

☐ My House

☐ My Friends

Word Check

Match the words to the pictures.

1 get away

2 sticky

3 shine

4 weak

a

b

c
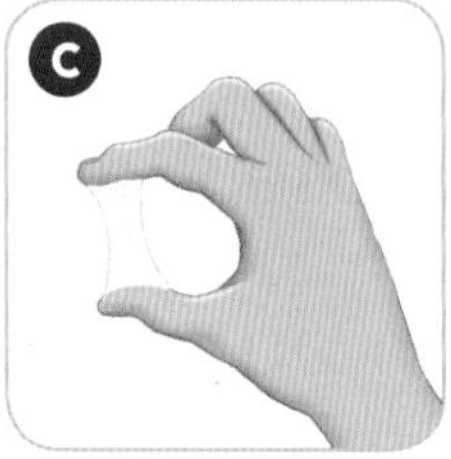

d

Grammar Check

Look at the pictures and circle the correct words.

1 

The butterfly (can / can't) get away.

2 

I (can / can't) eat the ant.

3 

They can't (see / sees) my house.

Comprehension Check

Read and choose the best answer.

1 Who am I?

a 

b 

c 

2 The house catches insects because it is ___________.

a big

b weak

c sticky

3 The house catches ___________ and ___________.

a bees – ants

b butterflies – ants

c butterflies – bees

TRY IT

Read and choose the right word.

Sunny Day	Rainy Day
My house 1) ___________. Ants can't 2) ___________ my house.	My house is 3) ___________. My house can't 4) ___________ ants. I become hungry.

weak   shines   catch   see

REVIEW TEST

[1~5] Look at the pictures and write the right words.

scared	protect	shine	get away	sticky

1

2

3

4
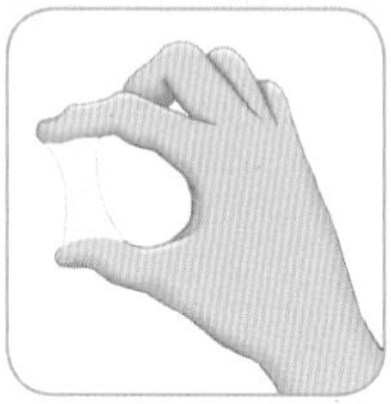

5

[6~10] Choose and write the correct word.

6 My house shines on a (weak / sunny) day. ______________

7 You (bring / get away) me delicious food. ______________

8 Rain makes my house (weak / protect). ______________

9 Friends help (shine / each other). ______________

10 Come here and (hide / scared) in me. ______________

[11~12] Look at the pictures and choose the correct words.

11 is scared   is hungry

The girl ________________.

12 can get away   can't get away

The man ________________.

[13~14] Read and answer.

My house is silver.
It shines on a sunny day.
Butterflies and ants can't see it.
My house is sticky.
It catches butterflies and ants.
They can't get away.
I eat them.
Rain makes my house weak.
Then it can't catch butterflies or ants.
So I become hungry!

13 Choose the words for the blanks.

My house is ___________ and ___________.

soft   sunny   sticky   silver

14 Check True or False.

a My house shines on a rainy day. True False

b My house can catch butterflies and ants. True False

c Wind makes my house weak. True False

당신의 글씨체는 어떤가요?

1. 글씨를 동글동글하게 쓰는 당신!

다른 사람들과 함께 경쟁하면서 공부하는 타입입니다.
도서관이나 독서실에서 여러 사람들의 공부하는 모습을
보며 공부해야 효과적입니다.

2. 글씨를 네모 반듯하게 쓰는 당신!

시끄러운 것을 싫어하고 혼자서 조용히 집중하는 것을 좋아하는
타입입니다. 독서실처럼 사람이 많은 곳보다는 집에서
혼자 공부해야 공부가 잘 됩니다.

3. 글씨를 날려 쓰는 당신!

벼락치기로 공부해야 공부가 잘 되는 독특한 타입입니다.
하지만 시험 전날에 무리하면 정작 시험 당일에는 졸려서
집중이 안 되는 등 부작용이 발생할 수 있습니다.
공부 스타일을 바꿔보는 건 어떨까요?

4. 상황에 따라 글씨가 변하는 당신!

특별히 자신의 공부 스타일이라는 것이 없네요. 공부를
좀 더 잘하고 싶다면 지금부터라도 나만의 공부 스타일을
만드는 것이 좋답니다.

UNIT 06 SCHOOL LIFE

Read and guess the stories.

STORY 01

Words to Learn Look at the pictures and read the words.

sweep

wipe

empty

trash can

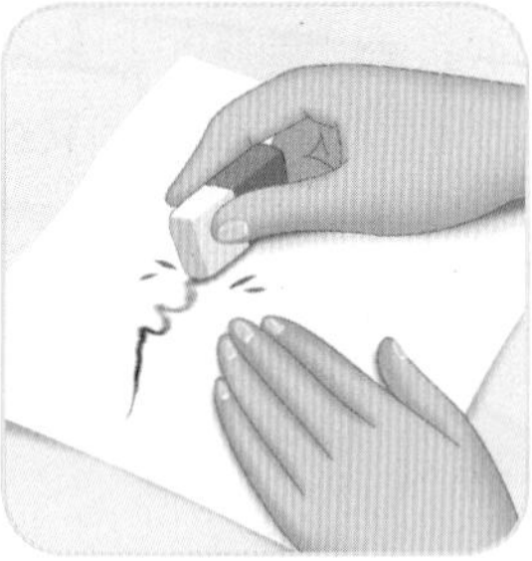
erase

plant

Grammar to Learn Look at the picture and read the sentences.

It's time to	clean the classroom.
	move the desks.

It's time to clean the classroom.

Move the desks and chairs.

Sweep the floor. **Wipe** the windows.

Empty the **trash can**. **Erase** the blackboard.

Water the **plants**. Feed the class fish.

Now the classroom is clean.

It's time to go home.

MAIN IDEA ☆☆

The best title is ________________.

- □ Cleaning the House
- □ Cleaning the Classroom

Word Check Choose the right picture for each word.

1 erase ______

2 sweep ______

3 wipe ______

4 empty ______

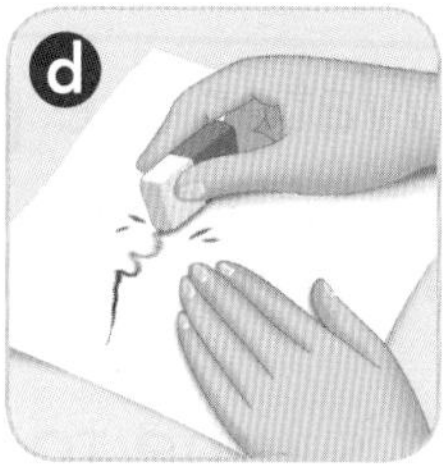

Grammar Check Look at the pictures and complete the sentences.

sweep water go

It's time to water the plant.

1

____________________ the floor.

2

____________________ home.

Comprehension Check

Read and choose the best answer.

1 The students ____________________.

a play soccer

b clean the classroom

c study very hard

2 What don't they do?

a 

b 

c 

3 The students __________ the plants and __________ the fish.

a water – feed

b wipe – empty

c sweep – move

TRY IT

Look at the pictures and choose the right word.

1) __________ the trash can.

2) __________ the plant.

3) __________ the blackboard.

erase

empty

water

STORY 02

Words to Learn

Look at the pictures and read the words.

get up

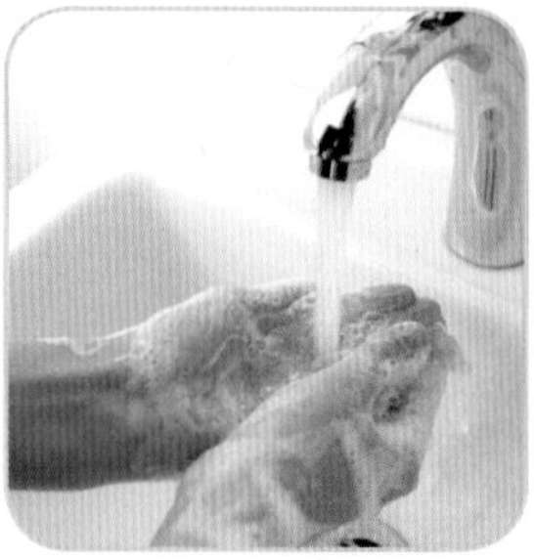

wash

get dressed

have breakfast

favorite

Grammar to Learn

Look at the pictures and read the sentences.

Do you	wash your face?
Do we / they	get dressed?

Does she	get up early?
Does he	go to school?

Do you **get up** early?

No, I don't.

Does she **wash** her face?

No, she doesn't.

Does he **get dressed**?

No, he doesn't.

Do they **have breakfast**?

No, they don't.

Do they go to school?

No, they don't.

Today is Sunday. They can be lazy.

Sunday is their **favorite** day!

MAIN IDEA ☆☆

The best title is ______________________.

- ☐ Their Birthdays
- ☐ Their Favorite Day

Word Check

Match the words to the pictures.

1 wash   2 have breakfast   3 get up   4 get dressed

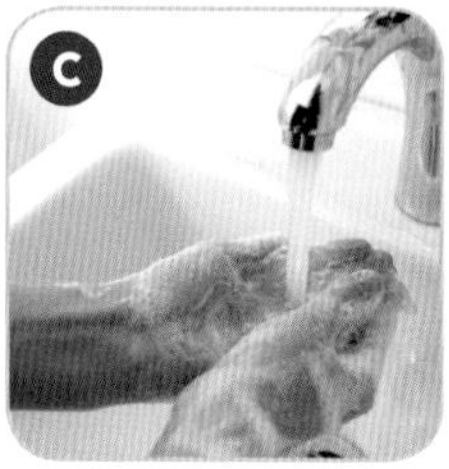

Grammar Check

Look at the example and complete the sentences.

You get up early.
➡ ___Do you get___ up early?

1 He gets dressed.
➡ ______________ dressed?

2 They have breakfast.
➡ ______________ breakfast?

3 Kate goes to the park.
➡ ______________ to the park?

Comprehension Check Read and choose the best answer.

1 They don't go to __________ today.

a school

b the park

c the hospital

2 They can be lazy today because ______________.

a today is Sunday

b today is holiday

c today is Christmas

3 Today is their ______________.

a holiday

b birthday

c favorite day

TRY IT Look at the pictures and fill in the blanks.

1) Q: ______________ her face? (wash)

A: No, she doesn't.

2) Q: ______________ breakfast? (have)

A: No, they don't.

REVIEW TEST

[1~5] Look at the pictures and write the right words.

sweep	get dressed	wash	erase	empty

1
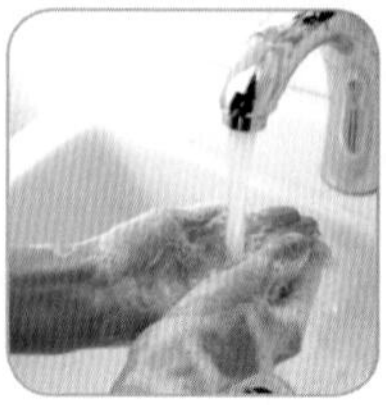

2
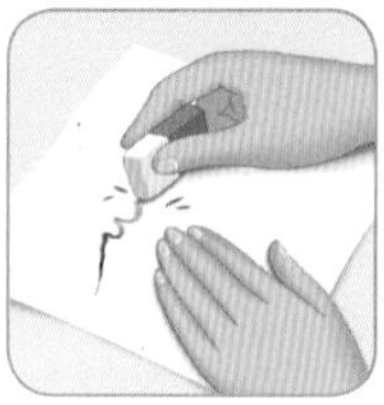

3

4

5

[6~10] Choose and write the correct word.

6 Saturday is my (favorite / erase) day. ____________

7 Let's (wipe / get up) the windows. ____________

8 I don't (empty / have breakfast) on Sundays. ____________

9 Empty the (sweep / trash can). ____________

10 She doesn't (get up / favorite) early. ____________

[11~12] Complete the sentences.

11 Q: ________________ clean the classroom?

A: No, they don't.

12 Q: ________________ have a brother?

A: No, she doesn't.

[13~14] Read and answer.

Do you get up early?
No, I don't.
Does she wash her face?
No, she doesn't.
Does he get dressed?
No, he doesn't.
Do they have breakfast?
No, they don't.
Do they go to school?
No, they don't.
Today is Sunday. They can be lazy.
Sunday is their favorite day!

13 They like Sundays because they can be ___________.

a lazy   b safe   c perfect

14 Check True or False.

a She doesn't wash her face.	True	False
b He doesn't get dressed.	True	False
c They have breakfast.	True	False

숫자 퀴즈 도전!

IQ가 높은 사람들만 가입할 수 있는 멘사 시험에 출제되는 문제입니다.
다음 퀴즈를 풀어보고 멘사 회원에 도전해 보세요!

1 단계

5 + 2 = 37

8 + 2 = 610

9 + 6 = 315

6 + 2 = 48

7 + 3 = ☐

2 단계

16 + 9 = 1

8 + 6 = 2

14 + 13 = 3

7 + 7 = ☐

1단계> 두 숫자를 뺀 값은 앞쪽에, 더한 값은 뒤에 넣으면 됩니다. 그래서 정답은 410!!
2단계> 이것은 시간 문제입니다. 예를 들어 16시+9시는 25시, 즉 1시죠. 그래서 정답은 2!!

UNIT 07
SAVE THE EARTH
Read and guess the stories.
Don't break my home.
Don't visit my home.
Thank you,
my friends!
Let's recycle! Let's put plastic, cans, and paper in the boxes.
PLASTIC
CAN
PAPER

STORY 01

Words to Learn Look at the pictures and read the words.

action

save the Earth

bottle

waste

recycle

Grammar to Learn Look at the picture and read the sentences.

Let's	save the Earth.
	protect the Earth.

Small **actions** can **save the Earth**.

Put plastic in the red box.

Collect cans in the blue box.

Paper goes into the green box.

Bottles go into the yellow box.

These things are not **waste**.

We can use them again.

Let's **recycle**!

Let's protect the Earth!

Think!

What can we do for the Earth?

1. ____________________
2. ____________________
3. ____________________

MAIN IDEA ☆☆

The best title is ____________________.

☐ Let's Recycle

☐ Let's Clean the Classroom

Word Check

Match the words to the pictures.

1 waste

2 bottle

3 recycle

4 action

a

b

c

d

Grammar Check

Look at the example and complete the sentences.

save the Earth

➡ Let's save the Earth.

1 put bottles in the blue box

➡ ________________ bottles in the blue box.

2 collect cans in the box

➡ ________________ cans in the box.

3 use these things again

➡ ________________ these things again.

Comprehension Check

Read and choose the best answer.

1 Collect __________ in the green box.

a paper
b bottles
c plastic

2 Cans go into the __________ box.

a red
b blue
c green

3 They put plastic in the __________ box and bottles in the __________ box.

a red – yellow
b blue – green
c yellow – blue

TRY IT

Read and choose the right things in the boxes.

1) We can recycle ...	2) We can't recycle ...

tissues	broken glass	cans
paper boxes	plastic spoons	food waste

STORY 02

Words to Learn Look at the pictures and read the words.

polar bear

the North Pole

spend

visit

tour

break

Grammar to Learn Look at the pictures and read the sentences.

Break the ice.	**Don't break**	the ice.
Catch fish here.	**Don't catch**	fish here.

I'm a **polar bear**.

I live at **the North Pole**.

I catch fish in the sea.

I **spend** my day on the ice.

Many people **visit** the North Pole these days.

They **tour** by ship.

Their ship **break**s the ice.

Don't break the ice!

Don't visit the North Pole!

MAIN IDEA ☆☆

The best title is ________________.

□ Visit the North Pole

□ Protect the North Pole

Word Check Choose the right picture for each word.

1 polar bear ______ 2 visit ______ 3 break ______ 4 tour ______

a 
b 
c 
d 

Grammar Check Look at the pictures and complete the sentences.

break the ice
➡ ___Don't break___ the ice.

1 catch fish here
➡ ______________ fish here.

2 tour by ship
➡ ______________ by ship.

Comprehension Check

Read and choose the best answer.

1 The polar bear spends its day on the ________.

a sea
b ice
c rocks

2 Many people visit the North Pole by ________.

a ship
b train
c airplane

3 The polar bear is angry because people ____________.

a catch fish
b break the ice
c spend time on the ice

TRY IT

Read and fill in the blanks.

The polar bear's worries		The polar bear's hopes
Many people visit the North Pole.	➡	1) ____________ the North Pole. (visit)
Their ship breaks the ice.	➡	2) ____________ the ice. (break)

REVIEW TEST

[1~5] Look at the pictures and write the right words.

polar bear visit recycle save the Earth spend

1

2

3

4

5

[6~10] Choose and write the correct word.

6 We can recycle the (bottles / visit). ____________

7 Small (actions / catches) can save the Earth. ____________

8 People (tour / action) by ship. ____________

9 Put the (waste / spend) in the trash can. ____________

10 Don't (bottle / break) the ice. ____________

[11~12] Look at the pictures and choose the right word.

11 Let Let's Let is

__________ clean the park.

12 Not Don't Doesn't

__________ visit the park.

[13~14] Read and answer.

Small actions can save the Earth.
Put plastic in the red box.
Collect cans in the blue box.
Paper goes into the green box.
Bottles go into the yellow box.
These things are not waste.
We can ______________.
Let's recycle.
Let's protect the Earth.

13 We can __________ plastic, cans, paper and bottles.

a buy
b recycle
c protect

14 Choose the words for the blank.

a use them again
b sell them again
c buy them again

깜짝 놀랄 우리 몸의 비밀!

우리 몸에 이런 비밀이? 우리 몸에 숨겨진 재미있는 사실을 알아봅시다!

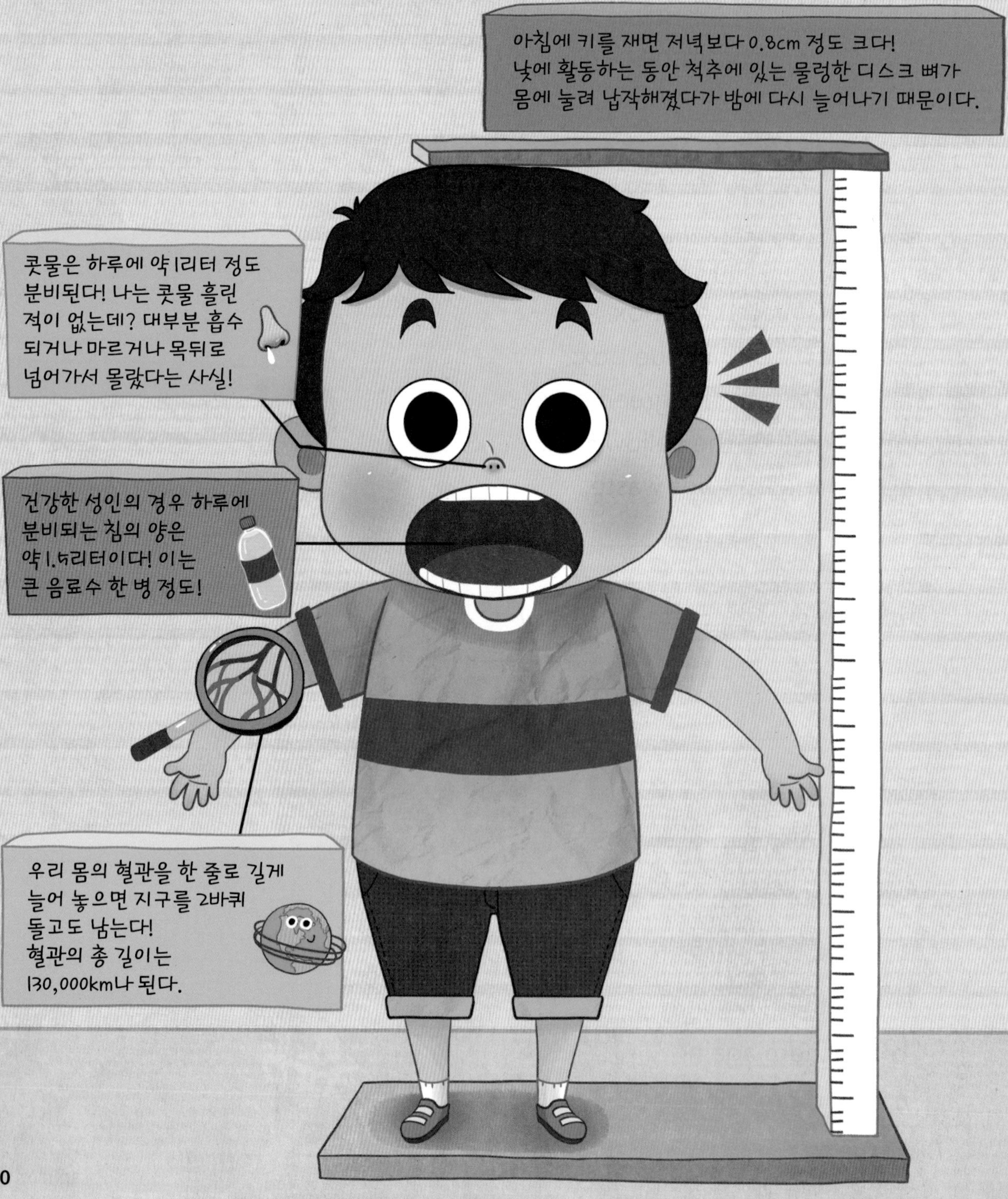

UNIT 08

FAIRY TALES

Read and guess the stories.

STORY 01

Words to Learn Look at the pictures and read the words.

be lost

woods

cold

yummy

bread

Grammar to Learn Look at the pictures and read the sentences.

There is	a house.
	a window.

There are	two houses.
	three windows.

It's Hansel and Gretel.

They **are lost** in the **woods**.

They are **cold** and hungry.

"There is a house!"

The house looks strange,

but it also looks **yummy**.

There is a chocolate door.

There are candy windows.

There are **bread** walls.

They eat the house.

Where is the house now?

배경지식

동화 「헨젤과 그레텔」에서 과자로 만든 집은 마녀가 헨젤과 그레텔을 잡아 먹기 위해 만들어 놓은 함정이었습니다. 과자 집으로 헨젤과 그레텔을 살찌워 잡아 먹을 계획이었답니다. 하지만 헨젤과 그레텔은 꾀를 내어 마녀를 물리치고 집으로 무사히 돌아옵니다.

MAIN IDEA ☆☆

The best title is ________________.

☐ A Yummy Woods

☐ A Yummy House

Word Check

Match the words to the pictures.

1 woods   2 cold   3 bread   4 yummy

Grammar Check

Circle the correct word for each sentence.

1 There (is / are) three notebooks.

2 There (is / are) a house.

3 There (is / are) some cookies.

4 There (is / are) two windows.

5 There (is / are) a door.

Comprehension Check Read and choose the best answer.

1 Hansel and Gretel are lost in the ________.

a town

b woods

c market

2 Read and match the words about the house.

a door •	• ① candy
b window •	• ② chocolate
c wall •	• ③ bread

3 Hansel and Gretel ________ the house.

a buy

b eat

c build

TRY IT Number the sentences in the correct order.

__1__ Hansel and Gretel are lost in the woods.

1) ______ Hansel and Gretel find a house.

2) ______ Hansel and Gretel eat the house.

3) ______ Hansel and Gretel are hungry.

STORY 02

Words to Learn

Look at the pictures and read the words.

magic

lamp

wish

comic book

cozy

Grammar to Learn

Look at the pictures and read the sentences.

Here is	a pizza.
	a book.

Here are	two pizzas.
	three books.

Genie : I'm Genie from the **magic lamp**.

Make three **wish**es.

Boy : I want some food.

Genie : POP! Here is a pizza for you.

Boy : I want some fun.

Genie : POP! Here are some **comic books** for you.

Boy : I want some sleep.

Genie : POP! Here is a **cozy** bed for you.

Sweet dreams!

MAIN IDEA

The best title is ______________.

☐ Three Wishes

☐ Three Magic Lamps

Word Check Choose the right picture for each word.

1 cozy ______

2 wish ______

3 magic ______

4 lamp ______

a

b

c

d

Grammar Check Circle the correct word for each sentence.

1 (Here is / Here are) two lamps.

2 (Here is / Here are) a bed.

3 (Here is / Here are) three books.

4 (Here is / Here are) a yummy pizza.

5 (Here is / Here are) some wishes.

Comprehension Check Read and choose the best answer.

1 Genie is from ______________.

a a dream

b a comic book

c a magic lamp

2 The boy can make __________ wishes.

a two

b three

c four

3 The boy gets a pizza, comic books, and a __________.

a bed

b lamp

c friend

TRY IT Read and fill in the blanks.

The boy's Wishes		Genie's Gifts
The boy wants 1) __________.	➡	Genie gives the boy a pizza.
The boy wants 2) __________.	➡	Genie gives the boy comic books.
The boy wants 3) __________.	➡	Genie gives the boy a bed.

REVIEW TEST

[1~5] Look at the pictures and write the right words.

magic　　cold　　lamp　　be lost　　yummy

1

2

3

4

5

[6~10] Choose and write the correct word.

6 This (bread / lamp) is yummy. ____________

7 The bed is (cozy / wish). ____________

8 I like walking in the (doors / woods). ____________

9 You can make two (wishes / woods). ____________

10 He wants to read (lamps / comic books). ____________

[11~12] Choose the right words.

there is　　there are

11 ______________ a picture.

12 ______________ some books.

[13~14] Read and answer.

Genie: I'm Genie from the magic lamp.
Make three wishes.
Boy : I want some food.
Genie: POP! Here is a pizza for you.
Boy : I want some fun.
Genie: POP! Here are comic books for you.
Boy : I want some sleep.
Genie: POP! Here is a cozy bed for you.
Sweet dreams!

13 Genie's house is ______________.

a a cozy bed

b a magic lamp

c a cookie house

14 Check True or False.

a The boy gets some magazines for fun. True False

b The boy gets a hamburger for food. True False

c The boy gets a bed for sleep. True False

나도 몰랐던 나의 센스

1. 세상에서 가장 착한 사자는 무엇일까요?

2. 왕이 궁에 가기 싫을 때 하는 말은 무엇일까요?

3. 미소의 반대말은 무엇일까요?

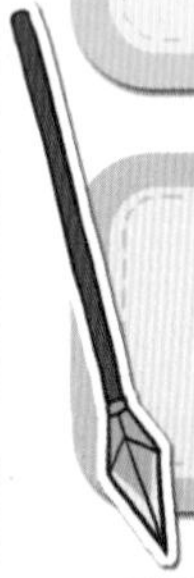

4. 날아온 창에 찔리려 할 때 옆 사람이 하는 말은 무엇일까요?

5. 사람이 죽어서 천사와 악마를 만났습니다.
천사와 악마에게 소원을 빌어 천국에 가야 합니다.
천사는 소원대로 이루어주고,
악마는 소원과 반대로 이루어준다고 합니다.
한가지 소원을 말해서
천국에 가는 법은 무엇일까요?

<정답>
1. 자원봉사자 2. 궁시렁 3. 당기소 4. 창피해! 5. "당신이사는 곳으로 가게해 주세요."라고 말한다.

초등학생의 영어 친구

리딩버디

정답 및 해석

1

UNIT 01 INTERESTING PLACES

STORY 01 PP. 8~11

Words to Learn

pilot: 조종사, 파일럿 castle: 성 wing: 날개 wall: 벽
museum: 박물관

Grammar to Learn

나는 천사이다.
우리는 / 당신들은 / 그들은 천사이다.
그는 / 그녀는 조종사이다.

직독직해 P. 9

My father is / a pilot.
나의 아빠는 ~이다 / 조종사
He is / in a paper airplane.
그는 있다 / 종이 비행기 안에
My mother is / a queen.
나의 엄마는 ~이다 / 여왕
She is / in a beautiful castle.
그녀는 있다 / 아름다운 성 안에
I am / an angel.
나는 ~이다 / 천사
I fly / with big wings.
나는 난다 / 큰 날개로
My brother and sister are / Spider-Man.
나의 남동생과 여동생은 ~이다 / 스파이더맨
They walk / on the wall.
그들은 걷는다 / 벽 위를
We are / in the Trick Eye Museum.
우리는 있다 / 트릭아이 박물관에

본문해석

나의 아빠는 조종사이다.
그는 종이 비행기에 있다.
나의 엄마는 여왕이다.
그녀는 아름다운 성 안에 있다.
나는 천사이다.
나는 큰 날개로 난다.
나의 남동생과 여동생은 스파이더맨이다.
그들은 벽 위를 걷는다.
우리는 트릭아이 박물관에 있다.

정답

MAIN IDEA

A Fun Museum

Word Check

1 ⓑ 2 ⓓ 3 ⓐ 4 ⓒ

Grammar Check

1 She is 2 He is 3 They are

1 그녀는 천사이다.
2 그는 조종사이다.
3 그들은 스파이더맨이다.

Comprehension Check

1 a 2 b 3 b

1 나의 아빠는 조종사이고 나는 천사이다.
2 나의 엄마는 성 안에 있다.
3 나의 남동생과 여동생은 벽 위를 걷는다.

TRY IT

1) wings 2) airplane 3) castle

나의 친구들과 나는 트릭아이 박물관에 있다.
나는 날개로 난다.
Lucy는 비행기에 있다.
Tom은 성 안에 있다.

STORY 02 PP. 12~15

Words to Learn

vacation: 휴가 hotel: 호텔 have a meal: 식사를 하다
take a shower: 샤워를 하다 feed: 먹이를 주다
safe: 안전한

Grammar to Learn

한 마리의 사자, 세 마리의 사자들
한 마리의 곰, 두 마리의 곰들
한 마리의 상어, 두 마리의 상어들
한 마리의 양, 두 마리의 양들

직독직해 P.13

Do you want / to have a special vacation?
당신은 원하나요 / 특별한 휴가 보내기를
Do you like / animals?
당신은 좋아하나요 / 동물을
Then / come / to our zoo hotel.
그렇다면 / 오세요 / 저희 동물원 호텔로
You can / have a meal / with lions.
당신은 ~할 수 있습니다 / 식사를 하다 / 사자와 함께
You can / take a shower / with bears.
당신은 ~할 수 있습니다 / 샤워를 하다 / 곰들과 함께
You can sleep / with sharks.
당신은 잘 수 있습니다 / 상어들과 함께
You can feed / giraffes / in your room.
당신은 먹이를 줄 수 있습니다 / 기린에게 / 당신의 방 안에서
But / don't worry.
하지만 / 걱정하지 마세요
It is / safe.
그것은 ~이다 / 안전한

본문해석

당신은 특별한 휴가를 보내길 원하나요?
당신은 동물들을 좋아하나요?
그렇다면 저희 동물원 호텔로 오세요.
당신은 사자들과 함께 식사할 수 있습니다.
당신은 곰들과 함께 샤워할 수 있습니다.
당신은 상어들과 함께 잘 수 있습니다.
당신은 당신의 방에서 기린들에게 먹이를 줄 수 있습니다.
하지만 걱정하지 마세요. 그것은 안전합니다.

정답

MAIN IDEA

An Interesting Hotel

Word Check

1 ⓓ 2 ⓐ 3 ⓑ 4 ⓒ

Grammar Check

1 giraffes 2 lions 3 sharks

1 당신은 기린과 함께 샤워를 할 수 있습니다.
2 당신은 당신의 방에서 사자에게 먹이를 줄 수 있습니다.
3 당신은 상어와 함께 식사를 할 수 있습니다.

Comprehension Check

1 b 2 b 3 b

1 이 호텔에는 사자들, 곰들, 상어들, 그리고 기린들이 있다.
2 당신은 곰들과 함께 샤워할 수 있다.
3 당신은 상어들과 함께 잘 수 있다.

TRY IT

1) have a meal 2) take a shower 3) feed

동물원 호텔을 방문하세요!
당신은 사자들과 함께 식사할 수 있습니다.
당신은 곰들과 함께 샤워할 수 있습니다.
당신은 기린들에게 먹이를 줄 수 있습니다.

REVIEW TEST PP.16~17

1 have a meal 2 museum 3 take a shower
4 safe 5 vacation 6 castle 7 wings
8 pilot 9 wall 10 feed 11 are 12 giraffes
13 a True b False 14 a

1 have a meal: 식사를 하다
2 museum: 박물관
3 take a shower: 샤워를 하다
4 safe: 안전한
5 vacation: 휴가
6 그 여왕은 성 안에 있다.
7 천사들은 큰 날개로 난다.
8 나의 남동생은 조종사가 되고 싶어한다.
9 스파이더맨은 벽 위를 걷는다.
10 나는 곰들에게 먹이를 줄 수 있다.
11 우리는 박물관에 있다.
12 당신은 기린들에게 먹이를 줄 수 있다.
13 a 당신은 곰들과 함께 샤워를 할 수 있다.
b 당신은 당신의 방에서 상어에게 먹이를 줄 수 있다.

UNIT 02 HEALTH

STORY 01 PP. 20~23

Words to Learn

itchy: 가려운 peanut: 땅콩 dangerous: 위험한
see a doctor: 진찰을 받다 take medicine: 약을 복용하다

Grammar to Learn

나는 / 당신(들)은 / 우리는 복숭아를 먹지 않는다.
그는 / 그녀는 / 그들은 새우를 먹지 않는다.

직독직해 P. 21

Bill / doesn't eat / peaches.
Bill은 / 먹지 않는다 / 복숭아를
His fingers / become itchy.
그의 손가락들은 / 가려워진다
His sister / doesn't eat / shrimps.
그의 여동생은 / 먹지 않는다 / 새우를
Her lips / become big.
그녀의 입술은 / 붓는다
His twin brothers / don't eat / peanuts.
그의 쌍둥이 남동생들은 / 먹지 않는다 / 땅콩을
Their cheeks / become red.
그들의 볼은 / 빨개진다
These are / allergies!
이것들은 ~이다 / 알레르기
They / can be dangerous.
그것들은 / 위험할 수 있다
See a doctor / quickly / and / take medicine.
진찰을 받아라 / 빨리 / 그리고 / 약을 복용해라

본문해석

Bill은 복숭아를 먹지 않는다.
그의 손가락들은 가려워진다.
그의 여동생은 새우를 먹지 않는다.
그녀의 입술은 붓는다.
그의 쌍둥이 남동생들은 땅콩을 먹지 않는다.
그들의 볼은 빨개진다.
이것들은 알레르기이다!
그것들은 위험할 수 있다.
빨리 진찰을 받고 약을 복용해라.

정답

MAIN IDEA

Dangerous Allergies

Word Check

1 ⓐ 2 ⓓ 3 ⓑ 4 ⓒ

Grammar Check

1 don't 2 doesn't 3 don't 4 don't 5 doesn't

1 나는 새우를 먹지 않는다.
2 그는 알레르기를 가지고 있지 않다.
3 당신은 복숭아를 먹지 않는다.
4 그들은 약을 복용하지 않는다.
5 James는 진찰을 받지 않는다.

Comprehension Check

1 c 2 a 3 c

1 복숭아는 Bill의 손가락들을 가렵게 만든다.
2 Bill의 여동생은 새우에 알레르기를 가지고 있다.
3 알레르기는 위험할 수 있다.

TRY IT

1) itchy 2) big 3) red

Bill의 손가락들을 가려워진다.
Bill의 여동생의 입술은 붓는다.
Bill의 남동생들의 볼은 빨개진다.

STORY 02 PP. 24~27

Words to Learn

gain weight: 살이 찌다 plate: 접시 taste: ~한 맛이 나다
exercise: 운동 forget: 잊다 hunger: 배고픔

Grammar to Learn

적게 먹어라.
운동을 해라.
자전거를 타라.

직독직해 P.25

I love / eating.
나는 매우 좋아한다 / 먹는 것을
Everything is delicious / to me.
모든 것은 맛있다 / 나에게
But / I don't want / to gain weight.
하지만 / 나는 원하지 않는다 / 살이 찌는 것을
How / can I / eat less?
어떻게 / 내가 ~할 수 있을까 / 덜 먹다
Put your food / on a blue plate.
음식을 두어라 / 파란 접시 위에
It / doesn't look delicious.
그것은 / 맛있어 보이지 않는다
Brush / your teeth.
닦아라 / 당신의 이를
The food / doesn't taste good.
음식은 / 맛있지 않다
Do / some exercises.
해라 / 약간의 운동을
You can forget / your hunger.
당신은 잊을 수 있다 / 당신의 배고픔을

본문해석

나는 먹는 것을 매우 좋아해요.
모든 것은 나에게 맛있어요.
하지만 나는 살이 찌는 것을 원하지 않아요.
내가 어떻게 덜 먹을 수 있을까요?
파란 접시에 당신의 음식을 놓으세요.
그것은 맛있어 보이지 않아요.
이를 닦으세요.
그 음식은 맛있지 않아요.
운동을 하세요.
당신은 배고픔을 잊을 수 있어요.

정답

MAIN IDEA

eating less

Word Check

1 ⓑ 2 ⓒ 3 ⓐ 4 ⓓ

Grammar Check

1 Brush 2 Do 3 Put

1 당신의 이를 닦아라.
2 운동을 해라.
3 접시 위에 사과들을 놓아라.

Comprehension Check

1 a 2 b 3 c

1 그 소녀는 덜 먹기를 원한다.
2 당신의 음식은 파란 접시 위에 있을 때 맛있어 보이지 않는다.
3 운동은 당신의 배고픔을 잊게 만들 수 있다.

TRY IT

1) a blue plate 2) my teeth 3) some exercises

당신은 덜 먹기를 원한다. 당신은 무엇을 할 수 있을까?
나는 파란 접시에 음식을 놓을 수 있다.
나는 나의 이를 닦을 수 있다.
나는 운동을 할 수 있다.

REVIEW TEST PP.28~29

1 gain weight 2 see a doctor
3 take medicine 4 peanut 5 dangerous
6 exercises 7 plate 8 itchy 9 taste
10 forget 11 Do 12 doesn't eat
13 a True b False c False 14 b

1 gain weight: 살이 찌다
2 see a doctor: 진찰을 받다
3 take medicine: 약을 복용하다
4 peanut: 땅콩
5 dangerous: 위험한
6 그들은 매일 운동을 한다.
7 나는 하얀 접시에 음식을 놓는다.
8 나의 손가락들은 가려워진다.
9 그 복숭아들은 맛있다.
10 나는 당신의 이름을 잊고 싶지 않다.
11 운동을 해라.
12 나의 남동생은 새우들을 먹지 않는다.
13 a 복숭아들은 Bill의 손가락들을 가렵게 만든다.
b 새우들은 Bill의 여동생의 입술을 빨갛게 만든다.
c 땅콩들은 Bill의 남동생들의 볼을 붓게 만든다.
14 그들은 알레르기가 있기 때문에 진찰을 받는다.

UNIT 03 SPECIAL JOBS

STORY 01 PP. 32~35

Words to Learn

perfect: 완벽한 lie down: 눕다, 누워 있다 leave: 떠나다
miss: 놓치다 chance: 기회

Grammar to Learn

나는 / 당신은 / 그녀는 잠을 잘 수 있다.
나는 / 당신은 / 그녀는 돈을 벌 수 있다.
우리는 / 당신들은 / 그들은 누울 수 있다.
우리는 / 당신들은 / 그들은 TV를 볼 수 있다.

직독직해 P. 33

Do you like / lying / in bed?
당신은 좋아하는가 / 누워 있는 것을 / 침대에
This job / is perfect / for you.
이 직업은 / 완벽하다 / 당신에게
Just lie down / in bed / all day.
단지 누워있기만 해라 / 침대에 / 하루 종일
You can sleep / 8 hours.
당신은 잘 수 있다 / 8시간 동안
You can play / games.
당신은 할 수 있다 / 게임을
You can watch / TV.
당신은 볼 수 있다 / TV를
But / you can't leave / the bed.
그러나 / 당신은 떠날 수 없다 / 침대를
You can get / 5,000 dollars / a month.
당신은 받을 수 있다 / 5000 달러를 / 한 달에
Don't miss / this chance.
놓치지 마라 / 이 기회를

본문해석

당신은 침대에 누워 있는 것을 좋아하나요?
이 직업은 당신에게 딱입니다.
하루 종일 침대에 누워 있기만 하세요.
당신은 8시간 동안 잘 수 있습니다.
당신은 게임을 할 수 있습니다.
당신은 TV를 볼 수 있습니다.
하지만 당신은 침대를 떠날 수는 없습니다.
당신은 한 달에 5,000달러를 벌 수 있습니다.
이 기회를 놓치지 마세요.

정답

MAIN IDEA

a job

Word Check

1 ⓒ 2 ⓐ 3 ⓑ 4 ⓓ

Grammar Check

1 can leave 2 can get

1 그는 침대를 떠난다.
그는 침대를 떠날 수 있다.
2 그들은 많은 돈을 번다.
그들은 많은 돈을 벌 수 있다.

Comprehension Check

1 b 2 c 3 c

1 이 직업에서, 당신은 하루 종일 침대에 누워 있을 수 있다.
2 당신은 한 달에 5,000 달러를 벌 수 있다.

TRY IT

1) sleep 8 hours, play games, watch TV
2) leave the bed

당신의 직업은 침대에 누워 있는 것이다.
1) 당신은 8시간 동안 잘 수 있다
당신은 게임을 할 수 있다
당신은 TV를 볼 수 있다
2) 당신은 침대를 떠날 수 없다

STORY 02 PP. 36~39

Words to Learn

pet: 애완동물 strange: 이상한 worried: 걱정하는
chew: 씹다 swallow: 삼키다

Grammar to Learn

내가 이상한가요?
당신이 예쁜가요?
그녀가 / 그가 걱정하나요?
우리는 / 그들은 행복한가요?

직독직해 P. 37

I eat / pet food.
나는 먹는다 / 애완동물 사료를
Am I / strange?
내가 ~인가 / 이상한
Well, / it is / my job.
음 / 그것은 ~이다 / 나의 직업
Pets eat / special food.
애완동물들은 먹는다 / 특별한 음식을
But like us, / pets enjoy / delicious food.
그러나 우리처럼 / 애완동물들은 즐긴다 / 맛있는 음식을
I taste / their food.
나는 맛본다 / 그들의 음식을
I find / the delicious food.
나는 찾는다 / 맛있는 음식을
Are you worried / about my health?
당신은 걱정하는가 / 내 건강에 대해
Don't worry. / I only chew / the food.
걱정하지 마라 / 나는 단지 씹는다 / 그 음식을
I don't swallow / it.
나는 삼키지 않는다 / 그것을

본문해석

나는 애완동물 사료를 먹습니다.
내가 이상한가요?
음, 그것은 나의 직업입니다.
애완동물들은 특별한 사료를 먹습니다.
하지만 우리처럼 애완동물도 맛있는 음식을 즐깁니다.
나는 그들의 사료를 맛봅니다.
나는 맛있는 사료를 찾습니다.
내 건강에 대해 걱정되나요?
걱정하지 마세요. 나는 그 사료를 씹기만 합니다.
나는 그것을 삼키지는 않습니다.

정답

MAIN IDEA

My Special Job

Word Check

1 ⓒ 2 ⓑ 3 ⓐ 4 ⓓ

Grammar Check

1 Are they happy? 2 Is he strange? 3 Am I lazy?

1 그들은 행복하다. / 그들은 행복한가요?
2 그는 이상하다. / 그가 이상한가요?
3 나는 게으르다. / 내가 게으른가요?

Comprehension Check

1 c 2 b 3 c

1 애완동물들은 맛있는 음식을 좋아한다.
2 그 남자는 애완동물을 위한 맛있는 사료를 찾는다.
3 그 남자는 애완동물 사료를 씹지만, 그것을 삼키지는 않는다.

TRY IT

1) taste 2) delicious food 3) worry about

나는 애완동물 사료 감별사이다.
나는 애완동물 사료를 맛본다.
나는 애완동물들을 위해 맛있는 사료를 찾는다.
나의 건강에 대해 걱정하지 말아라, 왜냐하면 나는 그것을 삼키지 않기 때문이다.

REVIEW TEST PP. 40~41

1 lie down 2 chance 3 leave 4 strange
5 pet 6 perfect 7 miss 8 worried 9 chew
10 swallow 11 can 12 Is she worried 13 b
14 a True b False c False

1 lie down: 눕다, 누워 있다
2 chance: 기회
3 leave: 떠나다
4 strange: 이상한
5 pet: 애완동물
6 이 직업은 당신에게 딱입니다.
7 이 기회를 놓치지 말아라.
8 나는 내 건강에 대해 걱정한다.
9 개들은 그 음식을 씹는다.
10 나는 애완동물 사료를 삼키지 않는다.
11 당신은 TV를 볼 수 있다.
12 그녀가 그 시험에 대해 걱정합니까?
13 그 남자의 직업은 애완동물 사료를 맛보는 것이다.
14 a 애완동물들은 특별한 애완동물 사료를 먹는다.
b 그 남자는 자신의 건강에 대해 걱정한다.
c 그 남자는 애완동물 사료를 삼킨다.

UNIT 04 HOBBIES

STORY 01 PP.44~47

Words to Learn

skate: 스케이트를 타다 jump: 뛰어오르다 pass: 지나가다
fall down: 넘어지다 hurt: 다치다

Grammar to Learn

나는 스케이트 타는 것을 좋아한다.
나는 인라인 스케이트를 가지고 있다.
나는 매일 스케이트를 타러 간다.
그는 스케이트 타는 것을 좋아한다.
그는 인라인 스케이트를 가지고 있다.
그는 매일 스케이트를 타러 간다.

직독직해 P.45

Amy loves / in-line skating.
Amy는 매우 좋아한다 / 인라인 스케이트 타는 것을
She skates / very well.
그녀는 스케이트를 탄다 / 매우 잘
She goes / very far.
그녀는 간다 / 매우 멀리
She jumps / very high.
그녀는 뛰어오른다 / 매우 높이
She passes everyone / very quickly.
그녀는 모든 사람을 지나간다 / 매우 빨리
CRASH!
쿵
She / falls down.
그녀는 / 넘어진다
She hurts / her arm.
그녀는 다친다 / 그녀의 팔을
She goes / to the hospital.
그녀는 간다 / 병원에
She says goodbye / to her in-line skates.
그녀는 작별 인사를 한다 / 그녀의 인라인 스케이트에게

본문해석

Amy는 인라인 스케이트 타는 것을 매우 좋아한다.
그녀는 스케이트를 매우 잘 탄다.
그녀는 매우 멀리 간다.
그녀는 매우 높이 뛰어오른다.
그녀는 매우 빨리 모든 사람을 지나간다.
쿵!
그녀는 넘어진다.
그녀는 팔을 다친다.
그녀는 병원에 간다.
그녀는 그녀의 인라인 스케이트에게 작별 인사를 한다.

정답

MAIN IDEA

Amy and Her In-line Skates

Word Check

1 ⓒ 2 ⓓ 3 ⓑ 4 ⓐ

Grammar Check

1 runs 2 skate 3 goes 4 passes 5 say

1 Amy는 멀리 달린다.
2 나는 스케이트를 매우 잘 탄다.
3 그녀는 서점에 간다.
4 그는 모두를 빨리 지나간다.
5 그들은 그들의 친구들에게 작별인사를 한다.

Comprehension Check

1 b 2 a 3 b

1 Amy는 매우 높이 뛰어오른다.
2 Amy는 병원에 간다. 왜냐하면 그녀는 넘어지기 때문이다.
3 Amy는 그녀의 팔을 다친다.

TRY IT

1) 4 2) 3 3) 2 4) 5

Amy는 매우 빠르게 스케이트를 탄다.
1) Amy는 병원에 간다.
2) Amy는 그녀의 팔을 다친다.
3) Amy는 넘어진다.
4) Amy는 그녀의 인라인 스케이트에게 작별인사를 한다.

STORY 02 PP.48~51

Words to Learn

collect: 모으다 famous: 유명한 touch: 만지다, 건드리다

locked: 잠긴　unlock: (잠긴 것을) 열다

Grammar to Learn

나는 인형을 갖고 싶다.
나는 그것들을 가지고 놀고 싶다.
그는 장난감을 갖고 싶어한다.
그는 그의 장식장에 장난감을 놓고 싶어한다.

직독직해 P.49

My father is / 41 years old.
나의 아빠는 ~이다 / 41살
But / he still wants / to have toys.
그러나 / 그는 여전히 원한다 / 장난감을 갖기를
He collects them / in his cabinet.
그는 그것들을 모은다 / 그의 장식장 안에
They are / famous superheroes / and robots.
그것들은 ~이다 / 유명한 슈퍼 히어로 / 그리고 로봇들
They are / cool.
그것들은 ~이다 / 멋진
I want / to play with them.
나는 원한다 / 그것들을 가지고 놀기를
But / I can't / touch them.
그러나 / 나는 ~할 수 없다 / 그것들을 만지다
The cabinet / is always locked.
장식장은 / 항상 잠겨 있다
Dad / please unlock / the cabinet!
아빠 / 열어 주세요 / 장식장을

본문해석

나의 아빠는 41세이다.
하지만 그는 아직도 장난감을 갖고 싶어한다.
그는 그의 장식장 안에 그것들을 모은다.
그것들은 유명한 슈퍼 히어로와 로봇이다.
그것들은 멋지다. 나는 그것들을 갖고 놀고 싶다.
하지만 나는 그것들을 만질 수 없다.
장식장은 항상 잠겨 있다.
아빠, 제발 장식장을 열어주세요!

정답

MAIN IDEA

My Father Likes Toys

Word Check

1 ⓑ　2 ⓐ　3 ⓓ　4 ⓒ

Grammar Check

1 wants to unlock　2 want to play
3 wants to have

1 그는 그 장식장을 연다. / 그는 그 장식장을 열고 싶어한다.
2 나는 로봇들을 가지고 논다. / 나는 로봇들을 가지고 놀고 싶다.
3 그녀는 가방이 많다. / 그녀는 많은 가방을 가지고 싶어한다.

Comprehension Check

1 b　2 c　3 c

1 그 소년의 아빠는 장난감 모으는 것을 매우 좋아한다.
2 그 소년의 아빠는 그의 장식장에 장난감을 놓는다.

TRY IT

1) collects　2) play　3) locked

나의 아빠는 그의 장식장에 장난감을 모은다.
나는 그것들을 가지고 놀고 싶지만, 나는 할 수 없다.
그 장식장은 잠겨 있다.

REVIEW TEST PP. 52~53

1 touch　2 fall down　3 skate　4 unlock
5 locked　6 jumps　7 collects　8 famous
9 pass　10 hurts　11 goes　12 want to
13 a　14 a True　b False　c False

1 touch: 만지다, 건드리다
2 fall down: 넘어지다
3 skate: 스케이트를 타다
4 unlock: (잠긴 것을) 열다
5 locked: 잠긴
6 Tom은 매우 높이 뛰어오른다.
7 Amy는 장난감들을 모은다.
8 그것들은 유명한 슈퍼 히어로들이다.
9 나는 빨리 모든 사람들을 지나간다.
10 나의 아빠는 그의 팔을 다친다.
11 그녀는 병원에 간다.
12 나는 컴퓨터 게임을 하고 싶다.
13 그의 아빠의 취미는 장난감을 모으는 것이다.
14 a 소년의 아빠는 유명한 로봇들을 모은다.
b 그 소년은 그의 아빠의 장난감을 가지고 놀 수 있다.
c 그 장식장은 언제나 열려 있다.

UNIT 05 NATURE

STORY 01 PP. 56~59

Words to Learn

scared: 무서워하는, 겁먹은 hide: 숨다
protect: 보호하다 bring: 가져다주다 each other: 서로

Grammar to Learn

그는 배고프다.
나는 무섭다.
나는 맛있는 음식을 원한다.
너는 좋은 친구이다.

직독직해 P. 57

Hey, / are you okay?
이봐 / 너 괜찮니
I am / very scared.
나는 ~이다 / 매우 무서운
A hungry fish wants / to eat me.
배고픈 물고기는 원한다 / 나를 먹기를
Come here / and hide / in me.
와라 여기로 / 그리고 숨어라 / 내 속에
I can protect / you.
나는 보호할 수 있다 / 너를
Thank you.
고마워
You always help / me.
너는 항상 돕는다 / 나를
You're welcome!
천만에
You help / me, / too.
너는 돕는다 / 나를 / 또한
You bring / me / delicious food.
너는 가져다준다 / 나에게 / 맛있는 음식을
We help / each other.
우리는 돕는다 / 서로를
We are / good friends.
우리는 ~이다 / 좋은 친구

본문해석

말미잘 : 이봐, 괜찮아?
흰동가리: 나 매우 무서워. 배고픈 물고기가 나를 먹고 싶어해.
말미잘 : 이리 와서 내 속에 숨어. 내가 너를 보호해줄 수 있어.
흰동가리: 고마워. 너는 언제나 나를 도와주는구나.
말미잘 : 천만에! 너도 나를 도와주잖아. 너는 내게 맛있는 음식을 가져다 주잖아.
흰동가리: 우리는 서로를 도와줘. 우리는 좋은 친구들이야.

정답

MAIN IDEA

Good Friends

Word Check

1 ⓒ 2 ⓐ 3 ⓑ 4 ⓓ

Grammar Check

1 hungry 2 delicious 3 scared

1 그 소년은 배가 고프다.
2 나는 맛있는 음식을 요리할 수 있다.
3 그들은 매우 겁먹었다.

Comprehension Check

1 c 2 a 3 c

1 물고기는 겁을 먹었다, 왜냐하면 배고픈 물고기가 자신을 먹고 싶어하기 때문이다.
2 물고기는 자신의 친구에게 음식을 준다.
3 그들은 좋은 친구들이다, 왜냐하면 그들은 서로를 도와주기 때문이다.

TRY IT

1) protect 2) bring 3) help

너는 나를 보호해준다.
너는 나에게 음식을 가져다준다.
우리는 서로를 돕는다.

STORY 02 PP.60~63

Words to Learn

shine: 반짝이다 sunny: 화창한 sticky: 끈적거리는

get away: 탈출하다, 벗어나다 weak: 약한

Grammar to Learn

우리는 움직일 수 없다.
우리는 탈출할 수 없다.
나는 그들을 잡을 수 없다.
나는 그들을 먹을 수 없다.

직독직해 P. 61

My house is / silver.
내 집은 ~이다 / 은빛의
It shines / on a sunny day.
이것은 반짝인다 / 화창한 날에
Butterflies and ants / can't see / it.
나비와 개미는 / 볼 수 없다 / 그것을
My house is / sticky.
내 집은 ~이다 / 끈적거리는
It catches / butterflies and ants.
이것은 잡는다 / 나비와 개미를
They / can't get away.
그들은 / 도망갈 수 없다.
And / I eat / them.
그리고 / 나는 먹는다 / 그들을
Rain makes / my house / weak.
비는 만든다 / 내 집을 / 약하게
Then / it can't catch / butterflies or ants.
그러면 / 이것은 잡을 수 없다 / 나비나 개미를
So / I become hungry!
그래서 / 나는 배고파진다

본문해석

내 집은 은빛이다.
그것은 화창한 날에는 반짝인다.
나비와 개미들은 그것을 볼 수 없다.
내 집은 끈적거린다.
이것은 나비와 개미를 잡는다.
그들은 탈출할 수 없다.
그리고 나는 그들을 먹는다.
비는 내 집을 약하게 만든다.
그러면 그것은 나비나 개미를 잡을 수 없다.
그래서 나는 배고파진다!

정답

MAIN IDEA

My House

Word Check

1 ⓑ 2 ⓒ 3 ⓐ 4 ⓓ

Grammar Check

1 can't 2 can't 3 see

1 나비는 탈출할 수 없다.
2 나는 개미를 먹을 수가 없다.
3 그들은 내 집을 볼 수가 없다.

Comprehension Check

1 a 2 c 3 b

1 나는 누구인가?
2 그 집은 곤충들을 잡을 수 있다, 왜냐하면 그것은 끈적거리기 때문이다.
3 그 집은 나비들과 개미들을 잡는다.

TRY IT

1) shines 2) see 3) weak 4) catch

화창한 날: 내 집은 반짝인다.
개미들은 내 집을 볼 수가 없다.
비 오는 날: 내 집은 약하다. 내 집은 개미를 잡을 수 없다. 나는 배고파진다.

REVIEW TEST PP. 64-65

1 shine 2 get away 3 protect 4 sticky
5 scared 6 sunny 7 bring 8 weak
9 each other 10 hide 11 is scared
12 can't get away 13 silver, sticky
14 a False b True c False

1 shine: 반짝이다
2 get away: 탈출하다, 벗어나다
3 protect: 보호하다
4 sticky: 끈적거리는
5 scared: 겁먹은
6 내 집은 화창한 날에 반짝인다.
7 너는 나에게 맛있는 음식을 가져다준다.
8 비가 내 집을 약하게 만든다.
9 친구는 서로를 돕는다.
10 이리 와서 내 속에 숨어.
11 소녀는 겁을 먹었다.
12 남자는 탈출할 수 없다.
13 내 집은 은빛이며 끈적거린다.
14 a 내 집은 비 오는 날에 반짝인다.
b 내 집은 나비와 개미를 잡을 수 있다.
c 바람은 내 집을 약하게 만든다.

UNIT 06 SCHOOL LIFE

STORY 01 PP. 68~71

Words to Learn

sweep: 쓸다 wipe: 닦다 empty: 비우다
trash can: 쓰레기통 erase: 지우다 plant: 식물

Grammar to Learn

교실을 청소할 시간이다.
책상을 옮길 시간이다.

직독직해 P. 69

It's time to clean / the classroom.
청소할 시간이다 / 교실을
Move / the desks and chairs.
옮겨라/ 책상과 의자를
Sweep / the floor.
쓸어라 / 바닥을
Wipe / the windows.
닦아라 / 창문을
Empty / the trash can.
비워라 / 쓰레기통을
Erase / the blackboard.
지워라 / 칠판을
Water / the plants.
물을 줘라 / 화분에
Feed / the class fish.
밥을 줘라 / 반 물고기에게
Now / the classroom is / clean.
이제 / 교실이 ~이다 / 깨끗한
It's time to go / home.
갈 시간이다 / 집에

본문해석

교실을 청소할 시간이다.
책상과 의자를 옮겨라.
바닥을 쓸어라. 창문을 닦아라.
쓰레기통을 비워라. 칠판을 지워라.
화분에 물을 줘라. 반 물고기에 밥을 줘라.
이제 교실이 깨끗하다.
집에 갈 시간이다.

정답

MAIN IDEA

Cleaning the Classroom

Word Check

1 ⓓ 2 ⓒ 3 ⓑ 4 ⓐ

Grammar Check

1 It's time to sweep 2 It's time to go

1 바닥을 쓸 시간이다
2 집에 갈 시간이다.

Comprehension Check

1 b 2 a, c 3 a

1 학생들은 교실을 청소한다.
2 그들은 무엇을 하지 않는가?
3 학생들은 화분에 물을 주고 물고기에게 밥을 준다.

TRY IT

1) Empty 2) Water 3) Erase

1) 쓰레기통을 비워라.
2) 식물에 물을 줘라.
3) 칠판을 지워라.

STORY 02 PP. 72~75

Words to Learn

get up: 일어나다 wash: 씻다 get dressed: 옷을 입다
have breakfast: 아침을 먹다 favorite: 가장 좋아하는

Grammar to Learn

너는 세수를 하니?
우리는 / 그들은 옷을 입니?
그녀는 일찍 일어나니?
그는 학교에 가니?

직독직해 P. 73

Do you / get up / early?
너는 ~하니 / 일어나다 / 일찍

No, / I don't.
아니 / 나는 아니야
Does she wash / her face?
그녀는 씻니 / 얼굴을
No, / she doesn't.
아니 / 그녀는 안 해
Does he get dressed?
그는 ~하니 / 옷을 입다
No, / he doesn't.
아니 / 그는 안 해
Do they have / breakfast?
그들은 먹니 / 아침식사를
No, / they don't.
아니 / 그들은 안 해
Do they go / to school?
그들은 가니 / 학교에
No, / they don't.
아니 / 그들은 안 해
Today is / Sunday.
오늘은 ~이다 / 일요일
They can be / lazy.
그들은 ~일 수 있어 / 게으른
Sunday is / their favorite day!
일요일은 ~이다 / 그들이 가장 좋아하는 날

본문해석

너는 일찍 일어나니?
아니, 나는 그렇지 않아.
그녀는 세수를 하니?
아니, 안 해.
그는 옷을 입니?
아니, 안 입어.
그들은 아침을 먹니?
아니, 안 먹어.
그들은 학교에 가니?
아니, 안 가.
오늘은 일요일이야. 그들은 게을러도 돼.
일요일은 그들이 가장 좋아하는 날이야!

정답

MAIN IDEA

Their Favorite Day

Word Check

1 ⓒ 2 ⓓ 3 ⓐ 4 ⓑ

Grammar Check

1 Does he get 2 Do they have 3 Does Kate go

1 그는 옷을 입는다.
그는 옷을 입니?
2 그들은 아침을 먹는다.
그들은 아침을 먹니?
3 Kate는 공원에 간다.
Kate는 공원에 가니?

Comprehension Check

1 a 2 a 3 c

1 그들은 오늘 학교에 가지 않는다.
2 그들은 오늘 게을러도 된다, 왜냐하면 오늘은 일요일이기 때문이다.
3 오늘은 그들이 가장 좋아하는 날이다.

TRY IT

1) Does she wash 2) Do they have

Q: 그녀는 세수를 하니?
A: 아니, 안 해.
Q: 그들은 아침을 먹니?
A: 아니, 안 먹어.

REVIEW TEST PP.76~77

1 wash 2 erase 3 empty 4 get dressed
5 sweep 6 favorite 7 wipe 8 have breakfast
9 trash can 10 get up 11 Do they
12 Does she 13 a 14 a True b True c False

1 wash: 씻다
2 erase: 지우다
3 empty: 비우다
4 get dressed: 옷을 입다
5 sweep: 쓸다
6 토요일은 내가 가장 좋아하는 날이다.
7 창문들을 닦자.
8 나는 일요일에 아침을 먹지 않는다.
9 쓰레기통을 비워라
10 그녀는 일찍 일어나지 않는다.
11 Q: 그들은 교실을 청소하니?
A: 아니, 그들은 안 해.
12 Q: 그녀는 남동생이 있니?
A: 아니, 그녀는 없어.
13 그들은 게으를 수 있기 때문에 일요일을 좋아한다.
14 a 그녀는 세수를 하지 않는다.
b 그는 옷을 입지 않는다.
c 그들은 아침을 먹는다.

UNIT 07 SAVE THE EARTH

STORY 01 PP. 80~83

Words to Learn

action: 행동 save the Earth: 지구를 구하다 bottle: 병
waste: 쓰레기 recycle: 재활용하다

Grammar to Learn

지구를 구하자.
지구를 보호하자.

직독직해 P. 81

Small actions can save / the Earth.
작은 행동들이 구할 수 있다 / 지구를
Put plastic / in the red box.
플라스틱을 넣어라 / 빨간 상자에
Collect cans / in the blue box.
캔을 모아라 / 파란 상자에
Paper goes / into the green box.
종이들은 들어간다 / 초록색 상자에
Bottles go / into the yellow box.
병은 들어간다 / 노란 상자에
These things are not / waste.
이것들은 ~가 아니다 / 쓰레기
We can use / them / again.
우리는 사용할 수 있다 / 그것들을 / 다시
Let's recycle!
재활용을 하자
Let's protect / the Earth!
보호하자 / 지구를

본문해석

작은 행동들이 지구를 구할 수 있습니다.
플라스틱은 빨간 상자에 넣으세요.
캔은 파란 상자에 모으세요.
종이는 초록색 상자에 들어갑니다.
병은 노란 상자에 들어갑니다.
이것들은 쓰레기가 아닙니다.
우리는 그것들을 다시 사용할 수 있습니다.
재활용을 합시다!
지구를 보호합시다!

정답

MAIN IDEA

Let's Recycle

Word Check

1 ⓓ 2 ⓐ 3 ⓑ 4 ⓒ

Grammar Check

1 Let's put 2 Let's collect 3 Let's use

1 병들을 파란 상자에 넣자.
2 캔을 상자에 모으자.
3 이 물건들을 다시 사용하자.

Comprehension Check

1 a 2 b 3 a

1 종이를 초록색 상자에 모아라.
2 캔은 파란 상자에 들어간다.
3 그들은 플라스틱을 빨간 상자에 병은 노란 상자에 넣는다.

TRY IT

1) can / paper boxes / plastic spoons
2) tissues / broken glass / food waste

1) 우리는 캔 / 종이 상자 / 플라스틱 숟가락을 재활용할 수 있다.
2) 우리는 휴지 / 깨진 유리 / 음식물 쓰레기는 재활용 할 수 없다.

STORY 02 PP. 84~87

Words to Learn

polar bear: 북극곰 the North Pole: 북극
spend: (시간 등을) 보내다 visit: 방문하다
tour: 여행하다 break: 깨뜨리다

Grammar to Learn

얼음을 깨시오.
여기서 낚시를 하시오.
얼음을 깨지 마시오.
여기서 낚시를 하지 마시오.

직독직해 P.85

I'm / a polar bear.
나는 ~이다 / 북극곰
I live / at the North Pole.
나는 산다 / 북극에
I catch / fish / in the sea.
나는 잡는다 / 물고기를 / 바다에서
I spend / my day / on the ice.
나는 보낸다 / 나의 하루를 / 얼음 위에서
Many people visit / the North Pole / these days.
많은 사람들이 방문한다 / 북극을 / 요즘
They tour / by ship.
그들은 여행한다 / 배로
Their ship breaks / the ice.
그들의 배는 깬다 / 얼음을
Don't break / the ice!
깨지 마라 / 얼음을
Don't visit / the North Pole!
방문하지 마라 / 북극을

본문해석

나는 북극곰입니다.
나는 북극에 삽니다.
나는 바다에서 물고기를 잡습니다.
나는 얼음 위에서 나의 하루를 보냅니다.
요즘 많은 사람들이 북극을 방문합니다.
그들은 배로 여행합니다.
그들의 배는 얼음을 깹니다.
얼음을 깨지 마세요!
북극에 오지 마세요!

정답

MAIN IDEA

Protect the North Pole

Word Check

1 ⓑ 2 ⓐ 3 ⓓ 4 ⓒ

Grammar Check

1 Don't catch 2 Don't tour

1 여기서 물고기를 잡지 마라.
2 배로 여행하지 마라.

Comprehension Check

1 b 2 a 3 b

1 그 북극곰은 얼음 위에서 하루를 보낸다.
2 많은 사람들이 배로 북극을 방문한다.
3 북극곰들은 화가 났다, 왜냐하면 사람들이 얼음을 깨기 때문이다.

TRY IT

1) Don't visit 2) Don't break

북극곰의 걱정: 많은 사람들이 북극을 방문한다. 그들의 배가 얼음을 깬다.
북극곰의 바람: 북극을 방문하지 말라. 얼음을 깨지 말라.

REVIEW TEST PP. 88-89

1 recycle 2 spend 3 save the Earth
4 polar bear 5 visit 6 bottles 7 actions
8 tour 9 waste 10 break 11 Let's
12 Don't 13 b 14 a

1 recycle: 재활용하다
2 spend: (시간 등을) 보내다
3 save the Earth: 지구를 구하다
4 polar bear: 북극곰
5 visit: 방문하다
6 우리는 병을 재활용할 수 있다.
7 작은 행동이 지구를 구할 수 있다.
8 사람들이 배를 타고 여행한다.
9 쓰레기를 쓰레기통에 넣어라.
10 얼음을 깨지 마라.
11 공원을 청소하자.
12 공원을 방문하지 마시오.
13 우리는 플라스틱, 캔, 종이 그리고 병을 재활용할 수 있다.

UNIT 08 FAIRY TALES

STORY 01 PP. 92~95

Words to Learn

be lost: 길을 잃다 woods: 숲 cold: 추운
yummy: 맛있는 bread: 빵

Grammar to Learn

집이 한 채 있다.
창문이 하나 있다.
집이 두 채 있다.
창문이 세 개 있다.

직독직해 P. 93

It's / Hansel and Gretel.
~이다 / 헨젤과 그레텔
They are lost / in the woods.
그들은 길을 잃었다 / 숲 속에서
They are / cold and hungry.
그들은 ~이다 / 춥고 배가 고프다
"There is / a house!"
~가 있다 / 집이 한 채
The house / looks strange,
그 집은 / 이상해 보인다
but / it / also / looks yummy.
하지만 / 그것은 / 또한 / 맛있어 보인다
There is / a chocolate door.
~가 있다 / 초콜릿 문이
There are / candy windows.
~가 있다 / 사탕 창문들이
There are / bread walls.
~가 있다 / 빵 벽들이
They eat / the house.
그들은 먹는다 / 집을
Where / is the house / now?
어디에 / 집이 있는가 / 이제

본문해석

헨젤과 그레텔이다.
그들은 숲 속에서 길을 잃었다.
그들은 춥고 배고프다.
"집 한 채가 있다!"
그 집은 이상해 보이지만,
또한 맛있어 보인다.
초콜릿으로 된 문이 있다.
사탕으로 된 창문들이 있다.
빵으로 된 벽들이 있다.
그들은 집을 먹는다.
이제 집이 어디에 있지?

정답

MAIN IDEA

A Yummy House

Word Check

1 ⓒ 2 ⓓ 3 ⓐ 4 ⓑ

Grammar Check

1 are 2 is 3 are 4 are 5 is

1 공책 세 권이 있다.
2 집 한 채가 있다.
3 쿠키가 몇 개 있다.
4 창문 두 개가 있다
5 문 하나가 있다.

Comprehension Check

1 b 2 a – ② b – ① c – ③ 3 b

1 헨젤과 그레텔이 숲속에서 길을 잃었다.
3 헨젤과 그레텔이 집을 먹는다.

TRY IT

1) 3 2) 4 3) 2

헨젤과 그레텔이 숲 속에서 길을 잃었다.
1) 헨젤과 그레텔이 집 한 채를 발견한다.
2) 헨젤과 그레텔이 집을 먹는다.
3) 헨젤과 그레텔은 배가 고프다.

STORY 02 PP. 96~99

Words to Learn

magic: 마술 lamp: 램프 wish: 소원

comic book: 만화책 cozy: 아늑한

Grammar to Learn

피자 한 판이 여기 있다.
책 한 권이 여기 있다.
피자 두 판이 여기 있다.
책 세 권이 여기 있다.

직독직해 P.97

I'm Genie / from the magic lamp.
나는 지니이다 / 요술램프에서 나온
Make / three wishes.
빌어라 / 세가지 소원을
I want / some food.
나는 원한다 / 음식을
POP! / Here is / a pizza / for you.
뻥! / 여기 있다 / 피자가 / 당신을 위한
I want / some fun.
나는 원한다 / 재미를
POP! / Here are / some comic books / for you.
뻥! / 여기 있다 / 만화책들이 / 당신을 위한
I want / some sleep.
나는 원한다 / 잠을
POP! / Here is / a cozy bed / for you.
뻥! / 여기 있다 / 아늑한 침대가 / 당신을 위한
Sweet dreams!
좋은 꿈을 꿔라

본문해석

지니: 저는 요술램프에서 나온 지니입니다.
세 가지 소원을 빌어보세요.
소년: 저는 음식을 원해요.
지니: 뻥! 당신을 위한 피자가 여기 있습니다.
소년: 저는 재미를 원해요.
지니: 뻥! 당신을 위한 만화책들이 여기 있습니다.
소년: 저는 잠을 원해요.
지니: 뻥! 당신을 위한 아늑한 침대가 여기 있습니다.
좋은 꿈 꾸세요!

정답

MAIN IDEA

Three Wishes

Word Check

1 ⓒ 2 ⓓ 3 ⓑ 4 ⓐ

Grammar Check

1 Here are 2 Here is 3 Here are 4 Here is
5 Here are

1 램프 두 개가 여기 있다.
2 침대 하나가 여기 있다.
3 책 세 권이 여기 있다.
4 맛있는 피자 한 판이 여기 있다.
5 소원들이 여기 있다.

Comprehension Check

1 c 2 b 3 a

1 지니는 요술램프에서 왔다.
2 그 소년은 세 가지 소원을 빌 수 있다.
3 그 소년은 피자, 만화책, 침대를 받는다.

TRY IT

1) (some) food 2) (some) fun 3) (some) sleep

그 소년은 음식을 원한다. ➡ 지니가 그 소년에게 피자를 준다.
그 소년은 재미있는 것을 원한다. ➡ 지니가 그 소년에게 만화책을 준다.
그 소년은 잠을 원한다. ➡ 지니가 그 소년에게 침대를 준다.

REVIEW TEST PP.100~101

1 yummy 2 magic 3 be lost 4 cold
5 lamp 6 bread 7 cozy 8 woods 9 wishes
10 comic books 11 There is 12 There are
13 b 14 a False b False c True

1 yummy: 맛있는
2 magic: 마법
3 be lost: 길을 잃다
4 cold: 추운
5 lamp: 램프
6 이 빵은 맛있다
7 그 침대는 아늑하다
8 나는 숲 속을 걷는 것을 좋아한다.
9 당신은 두 개의 소원을 빌 수 있다.
10 그는 만화책을 읽고 싶어한다.
11 그림 하나가 있다.
12 책 몇 권이 있다.
13 지니의 집은 요술램프이다.
14 a 그 소년은 재미있는 것으로 잡지를 받는다.
b 그 소년은 음식으로 햄버거를 받는다.
c 그 소년은 잠을 위해 침대를 받는다.

지은이

NE능률 영어교육연구소

NE능률 영어교육연구소는 혁신적이며 효율적인 영어 교재를 개발하고
영어 학습의 질을 한 단계 높이고자 노력하는 NE능률의 연구조직입니다.

리딩버디 1

펴 낸 이 주민홍
펴 낸 곳 서울특별시 마포구 월드컵북로 396(상암동) 누리꿈스퀘어 비즈니스타워 10층
㈜NE능률 (우편번호 03925)
펴 낸 날 2016년 1월 5일 개정판 제1쇄
2023년 4월 15일 제14쇄
전 화 02 2014 7114
팩 스 02 3142 0356
홈페이지 www.neungyule.com
등록번호 제 1-68호
I S B N 979-11-253-0969-7 63740
정 가 10,000원

NE 능률

고객센터

교재 내용 문의 : contact.nebooks.co.kr (별도의 가입 절차 없이 작성 가능)
제품 구매, 교환, 불량, 반품 문의 : 02-2014-7114
☎ 전화문의는 본사 업무시간 중에만 가능합니다.

초등학생의 영어 친구

리딩버디

단어장

1

NE 능률

UNIT 05 NATURE

듣고 따라 말해 봅시다.

scared [skɛərd] 무서워하는, 겁먹은

fish [fiʃ] 물고기

hide [haid] 숨다

protect [prətékt] 보호하다

help [help] 돕다

bring [briŋ] 가져다주다

each other [iːtʃ ʌ́ðər] 서로

silver [sílvər] 은빛의, 은색의

shine [ʃain] 반짝이다

sunny [sʌ́ni] 화창한

NE능률 교재 MAP

독해

아래 교재 MAP을 참고하여 본인의 현재 혹은 목표 수준에 따라 교재를 선택하세요.
NE능률 교재들과 함께 영어실력을 쑥쑥~ 올려보세요!
MP3 등 교재 부가 학습 서비스 및 자세한 교재 정보는 www.nebooks.co.kr 에서 확인하세요.

초1-2
- 초등영어 리딩이 된다 Start 1
- 초등영어 리딩이 된다 Start 2
- 초등영어 리딩이 된다 Start 3
- 초등영어 리딩이 된다 Start 4

초3
- 리딩버디 1

초3-4
- 리딩버디 2
- 초등영어 리딩이 된다 Basic 1
- 초등영어 리딩이 된다 Basic 2
- 초등영어 리딩이 된다 Basic 3
- 초등영어 리딩이 된다 Basic 4

초4-5
- 리딩버디 3
- 주니어 리딩튜터 스타터 1

초5-6
- 초등영어 리딩이 된다 Jump 1
- 초등영어 리딩이 된다 Jump 2
- 초등영어 리딩이 된다 Jump 3
- 초등영어 리딩이 된다 Jump 4
- 주니어 리딩튜터 스타터 2

초6-예비중
- 1316팬클럽 독해 1
- 주니어 리딩튜터 1
- Junior Reading Expert 1
- Reading Forward Basic 1

중1
- 주니어 리딩튜터 2
- Junior Reading Expert 2
- Reading Forward Basic 2
- 열중 16강 독해+문법 1
- Reading Inside Starter

중1-2
- 1316팬클럽 독해 2
- 주니어 리딩튜터 3
- 정말 기특한 구문독해 입문
- Junior Reading Expert 3
- Reading Forward Intermediate 1
- 열중 16강 독해+문법 2
- Reading Inside 1

중2-3
- 1316팬클럽 독해 3
- 주니어 리딩튜터 4
- 정말 기특한 구문독해 기본
- Junior Reading Expert 4
- Reading Forward Intermediate 2
- Reading Inside 2

중3
- 리딩튜터 입문
- 정말 기특한 구문독해 완성
- Reading Forward Advanced 1
- 열중 16강 독해+문법 3
- Reading Inside 3

중3-예비고
- Reading Expert 1
- 리딩튜터 기본
- Reading Forward Advanced 2

고1
- 빠바 기초세우기
- 리딩튜터 실력
- Reading Expert 2
- TEPS BY STEP G+R Basic

고1-2
- 빠바 구문독해
- 리딩튜터 수능 PLUS
- Reading Expert 3

고2-3, 수능 실전
- 빠바 유형독해
- 빠바 종합실전편
- Reading Expert 4
- TEPS BY STEP G+R 1

고3 이상, 수능 고난도
- Reading Expert 5
- 능률 고급영문독해

수능 이상/ 토플 80-89 · 텝스 600-699점
- ADVANCED Reading Expert 1
- TEPS BY STEP G+R 2
- RADIX TOEFL Blue Label Reading 1,2

수능 이상/ 토플 90-99 · 텝스 700-799점
- ADVANCED Reading Expert 2
- RADIX TOEFL Black Label Reading 1

수능 이상/ 토플 100 · 텝스 800점 이상
- RADIX TOEFL Black Label Reading 2
- TEPS BY STEP G+R 3

초등학생의 영어 친구

리딩버디

WORKBOOK

1

NE 능률

초등학생의 영어 친구

리딩버디

WORKBOOK

1

[1~2] Write the words correctly three times.

1  **alwl** ______ ______ ______

2  **usemum** ______ ______ ______

[3~5] Look at the pictures and choose the correct word.

castle	pilot	wing

3 

______

4 

______

5 

______

[6~8] Choose the correct word and write the complete sentence.

6 [I / He] is in an airplane. (그는 비행기 안에 있다.)

→ ______________________________

7 We [is / are] in the museum. (우리는 박물관 안에 있다.)

→ ______________________________

8 Tom [am / is] in a castle. (Tom은 성 안에 있다.)

→ ______________________________

[9~11] Match the sentence parts and write the complete sentences.

9  He is • • ⓐ Spider-Man.

10  She is • • ⓑ an angel.

11  They are • • ⓒ a pilot.

9 ______________________________

10 ______________________________

11 ______________________________

[1~3] Look at the pictures and complete the words.

f c a d e s

1  va___ ___tion

2  fe___ ___

3  ___a___e

[4~6] Look at the pictures and choose the correct word/phrase.

take a shower hotel have a meal

4 

____

5 

____

6 

____

[7~9] Choose the correct word and write the camplete sentence.

7 You can take a shower with [bear / bears]. (당신은 곰들과 샤워를 할 수 있다.)

→ ____________________

8 You can feed [giraffe / giraffes]. (당신은 기린들에게 먹이를 줄 수 있다.)

→ ____________________

9 You can sleep with [shark / sharks]. (당신은 상어들과 잘 수 있다.)

→ ____________________

[10~12] Match the sentence parts and write the complete sentences.

10  You can have • • ⓐ a meal with sharks.

11  You can feed • • ⓑ a shower with giraffes.

12  You can take • • ⓒ lions in your room.

10 ____________________

11 ____________________

12 ____________________

[1~2] Write the words correctly three times.

1 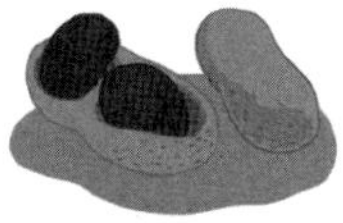 pantue ____________ ____________ ____________

2  adsenrgou ____________ ____________ ____________

[3~5] Look at the pictures and choose the correct word/phrase.

itchy	take medicine	see a doctor

3 
____

4 
____

5 
____

DATE PARENTS TEACHER

[6~8] Choose the correct word and write the complete sentence.

6 He [don't / doesn't] have allergies. (그는 알레르기를 가지고 있지 않다.)

→ ______________________________

7 They [don't / doesn't] take medicine. (그들은 약을 복용하지 않는다.)

→ ______________________________

8 James [don't / doesn't] see a doctor. (James는 진찰을 받지 않는다.)

→ ______________________________

[9~11] Match the sentence parts and write the complete sentences.

9  I • • ⓐ doesn't eat peaches.

10  Bill • • ⓑ don't eat shrimps.

11 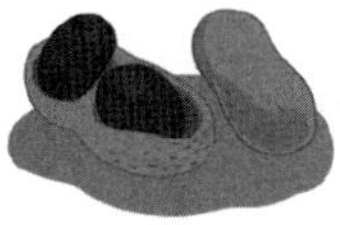 They • • ⓒ don't eat peanuts.

9 ______________________________

10 ______________________________

11 ______________________________

[1~3] Look at the pictures and complete the words.

h e g t o a r

1 

t____ s____ e

2 

f____ r____ ____ t

3 

____ u n g e ____

[4~6] Look at the pictures and choose the correct word/phrase.

exercise gain weight plate

4 

____

5 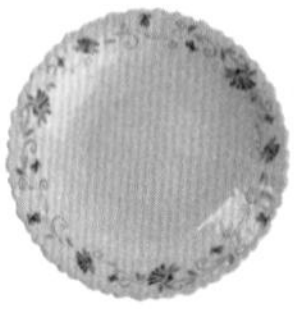

____

6 

____

DATE | PARENTS | TEACHER

[7~9] Choose the correct word and write the complete sentence.

7 [Eat / Eats] less. (더 적게 먹어라.)

→ ______________________________

8 [Brush / Brushes] your teeth. (이를 닦아라.)

→ ______________________________

9 [Ride / Rides] a bicycle. (자전거를 타라.)

→ ______________________________

[10~12] Match the sentence parts and write the complete sentences.

10  Brush • • ⓐ the apples on a plate.

11 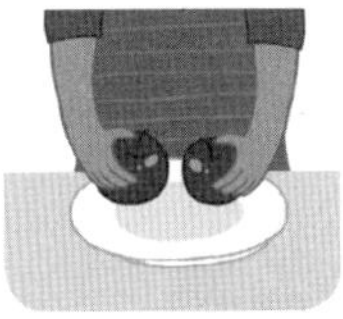 Put • • ⓑ some exercises.

12  Do • • ⓒ your teeth.

10 ______________________________

11 ______________________________

12 ______________________________

UNIT 03 ☆ SPECIAL JOBS STORY 01

[1~2] Write the words correctly three times.

1  smsi ______ ______ ______

2  preetfc ______ ______ ______

[3~5] Look at the pictures and choose the correct word/phrase.

leave	chance	lie down

3 

______

4 

______

5 

______

[6~8] Choose the correct word and write the complete sentence.

6 You [can / can't] play computer games. (당신은 컴퓨터 게임을 할 수 있다.)

→ ______________________________

7 They [can / can't] get money. (그들은 돈을 벌 수 있다.)

→ ______________________________

8 He can [leave, leaves] the bed. (그는 침대를 떠날 수 있다.)

→ ______________________________

[9~11] Match the sentence parts and write the complete sentences.

9  He can • • ⓐ watch TV.

10  I can • • ⓑ play games.

11 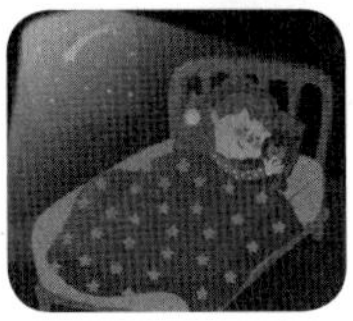 She can • • ⓒ sleep.

9 ______________________________

10 ______________________________

11 ______________________________

[1~2] Look at the pictures and complete the words.

a e h l w

1  c____ ____w

2  sw____ ____lo____

[3~5] Look at the pictures and choose the correct word.

strange pet worried

3  __________

4 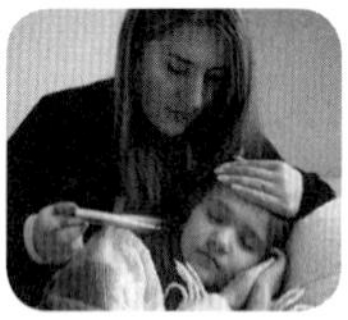 __________

5  __________

DATE PARENTS TEACHER

[6~8] Choose the correct word and write the complete sentence.

6 [She is, Is she] happy? (그녀는 행복한가요?)

→ ______________________________

7 [You are, Are you] worried about my health? (당신은 내 건강이 걱정되나요?)

→ ______________________________

8 [He is, Is he] strange? (그가 이상한가요?)

→ ______________________________

[9~11] Match the sentence parts and write the complete sentences.

9  Is he • • ⓐ happy?

10  Are you • • ⓑ strange?

11  Am I • • ⓒ worried about the test?

9 ______________________________

10 ______________________________

11 ______________________________

UNIT 04 ☆ HOBBIES STORY 01

[1 ~ 2] Write the words correctly three times.

1  **satek** ______________ ______________ ______________

2  **assp** ______________ ______________ ______________

[3 ~ 5] Look at the pictures and choose the correct word/phrase.

jump	hurt	fall down

3 

____

4 

____

5 

____

[6~8] Choose the correct word and write the complete sentence.

6 Amy [run / runs] far. (Amy는 멀리 달린다.)

→ ______________________________

7 She [go / goes] to the bookstore. (그녀는 서점에 간다.)

→ ______________________________

8 I [skate / skates] very well. (나는 스케이트를 매우 잘 탄다.)

→ ______________________________

[9~11] Match the sentence parts and write the complete sentences.

9  She • • ⓐ jumps very high.

10  He • • ⓑ passes her quickly.

11  She • • ⓒ likes skating.

9 ______________________________

10 ______________________________

11 ______________________________

[1~2] Look at the pictures and complete the words.

a o l e u m

1  c___l______ct

2  f______o___s

[3~5] Look at the pictures and choose the correct word.

locked touch unlock

3 

______

4 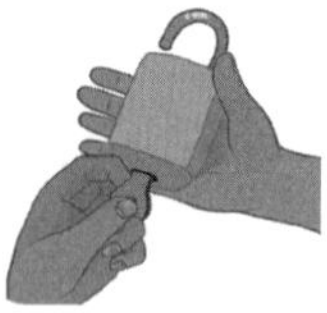

______

5 

______

[6~8] Choose the correct word and write the complete sentence.

6 I want [collect / to collect] superheroes. (나는 슈퍼 히어로들을 모으고 싶다.)

→ ______________________________

7 They want [play / to play] with robots. (그들은 로봇을 가지고 놀고 싶어한다.)

→ ______________________________

8 He wants [to unlock / to unlocks] the cabinet. (그는 그 장식장을 열고 싶어한다.)

→ ______________________________

[9~11] Match the sentence parts and write the complete sentences.

9  I want • • ⓐ to have toys.

10  She wants • • ⓑ to play with dolls.

11  He wants • • ⓒ to play computer games.

9 ______________________________

10 ______________________________

11 ______________________________

[1~3] Look at the pictures and complete the words.

b i c r e d n

1  hi___ ___

2  ___r___ ___g

3  s___a___ed

[4~5] Look at the pictures and choose the correct word/phrase.

protect each other

4 

____

5 

____

[6~8] Choose the correct word and write the complete sentence.

6 They are very [scared / delicious]. (그들은 매우 겁먹었다.)

→ ______________________________

7 You bring me [hungry / delicious] food. (너는 나에게 맛있는 음식을 가져다준다.)

→ ______________________________

8 The fish is [hungry / scared]. (그 물고기는 배가 고프다.)

→ ______________________________

[9~11] Match the sentence parts and write the complete sentences.

9  They are • • ⓐ delicious food.

10  She can cook • • ⓑ scared.

11  We are • • ⓒ good friends.

9 ______________________________

10 ______________________________

11 ______________________________

[1~3] Write the words correctly three times.

1 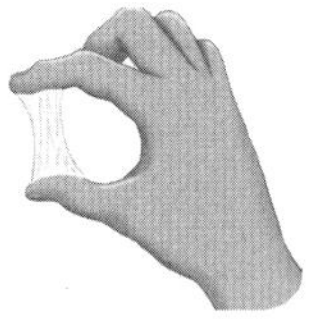 **ytskci** ______ ______ ______

2  **kwae** ______ ______ ______

3  **nynus** ______ ______ ______

[4~5] Look at the pictures and choose the correct word/phrase.

shine	get away

4 

______

5 

______

DATE PARENTS TEACHER

[6~8] Choose the correct word and write the complete sentence.

6 I [can / can't] eat an ant. (나는 개미를 먹을 수 없다.)

→ ______________________________

7 They [can / can't] see my house. (그들은 내 집을 볼 수 없다.)

→ ______________________________

8 The butterfly [can / can't] get away. (그 나비는 탈출할 수 없다.)

→ ______________________________

[9~10] Match the sentence parts and write the complete sentences.

9  We can't • • ⓐ catch them.

10  I can't • • ⓑ move.

9 ______________________________

10 ______________________________

UNIT 06 ☆ SCHOOL LIFE STORY 01

[1~3] Look at the pictures and complete the words.

e p w r s i

1 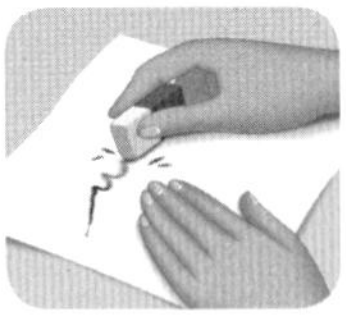 e____ a ____ e

2  s ____ e ____ p

3  w ____ ____ e

[4~6] Look at the pictures and choose the correct word/phrase.

empty trash can plant

4 
____

5 
____

6 
____

[7~9] Choose the correct word and write the complete sentence.

7 [It's time / It's time to] clean the classroom. (교실을 청소할 시간이다.)

→ ______________________________

8 [It's time / It's time to] water the plant. (식물에 물을 줄 시간이다.)

→ ______________________________

9 [It's time / It's time to] wipe the windows. (창문을 닦을 시간이다.)

→ ______________________________

[10~12] Match the sentence parts and write the complete sentences.

10  It's time • • ⓐ to go home.

11  It's time • • ⓑ to move the desks.

12  It's time • • ⓒ to sweep the floor.

10 ______________________________

11 ______________________________

12 ______________________________

UNIT 06 ☆ SCHOOL LIFE STORY 02

[1~2] Write the words correctly three times.

1 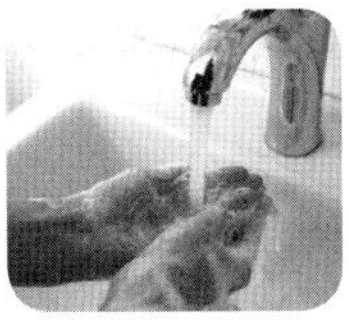 shaw ______ ______ ______

2  rovafite ______ ______ ______

[3~5] Look at the pictures and choose the correct phrase.

have breakfast	get up	get dressed

3 

______

4 

______

5 

______

[6~8] Choose the correct word and write the complete sentence.

6 [Do / Does] they clean the classroom? (그들은 교실을 청소하니?)

→ ______________________________

7 [Do / Does] she have a brother? (그녀는 남자 형제가 있니?)

→ ______________________________

8 [Do / Does] he get dressed? (그는 옷을 입니?)

→ ______________________________

[9~11] Match the sentence parts and write the complete sentences.

9  Do they • • ⓐ wash her face?

10  Does she • • ⓑ have breakfast?

11  Do you • • ⓒ get up early?

9 ______________________________

10 ______________________________

11 ______________________________

[1~2] Write the words correctly three times.

1  **cerycel** ______________ ______________ ______________

2  **nacito** ______________ ______________ ______________

[3~5] Look at the pictures and choose the correct word/phrase.

save the Earth	waste	bottle

3 

____

4 

____

5 

____

[6~8] Choose the correct word and write the complete sentence.

6 [Let / Let's] put bottles in the blue box. (병들을 파란 상자에 넣자.)

→ ______________________________

7 Let's [protect / protects] the Earth. (지구를 보호하자.)

→ ______________________________

8 [Let / Let's] use these things again. (이 물건들을 다시 사용하자.)

→ ______________________________

[9~10] Match the sentence parts and write the complete sentences.

9  Let's • • ⓐ collect cans in the box.

10 

Let's • • ⓑ clean the park.

9 ______________________________

10 ______________________________

[1~3] Look at the pictures and complete the words.

s d t p r n e

1  b___ ___ak

2  vi___ i___

3  s___ e___ ___

[4~6] Look at the pictures and choose the correct word/phrase.

polar bear tour the North Pole

4  __________

5  __________

6  __________

DATE PARENTS TEACHER

[7~9] Choose the correct word and write the complete sentence.

7 [Do / Don't] break the glass. (유리컵을 깨지 마라.)

→ ______________________________

8 [Don't / Doesn't] visit the North Pole. (북극을 방문하지 마라.)

→ ______________________________

9 [Do / Don't] tour by ship. (배로 여행하지 마라.)

→ ______________________________

[10~12] Match the sentence parts and write the complete sentences.

10 

Don't visit • • ⓐ fish here.

11 
Don't catch • • ⓑ the park.

12 
Don't break • • ⓒ the ice.

10 ______________________________

11 ______________________________

12 ______________________________

UNIT 08 ☆ FAIRY TALES STORY 01

[1~2] Write the words correctly three times.

1  **sdwoo** ____________ ____________ ____________

2  **drabe** ____________ ____________ ____________

[3~5] Look at the pictures and choose the correct word/phrase.

be lost	cold	yummy

3 

____

4 

____

5 

____

[6~8] Choose the correct word and write the complete sentence.

6 There [is / are] some cookies. (쿠키가 좀 있다.)

→ ______________________________

7 There [is / are] a door. (문 하나가 있다.)

→ ______________________________

8 There [is / are] three windows. (창문 세 개가 있다.)

→ ______________________________

[9~11] Match the sentence parts and write the complete sentences.

9  There are • • ⓐ yummy food.

10  There is • • ⓑ two houses.

11  There is • • ⓒ a window.

9 ______________________________

10 ______________________________

11 ______________________________

[1~2] Look at the pictures and complete the words.

m c a g

1  l___ ___p

2  ma___i___

[3~5] Look at the pictures and choose the correct word/phrase.

comic book wish cozy

3 

____

4 

____

5 

____

DATE PARENTS TEACHER

[6~8] Choose the correct word and write the complete sentence.

6 Here [is / are] three books. (책 세 권이 여기 있다.)

→ ______________________________

7 Here [is / are] a yummy pizza. (맛있는 피자 한 판이 여기 있다.)

→ ______________________________

8 Here [is / are] some wishes. (소원들이 여기 있다.)

→ ______________________________

[9~11] Match the sentence parts and write the complete sentences.

9  Here is • • ⓐ comic books.

10  Here is • • ⓑ a cozy bed.

11  Here are • • ⓒ a magic lamp.

9 ______________________________

10 ______________________________

11 ______________________________

★ 정답 ★

UNIT 01 ★ INTERESTING PLACES

STORY 01 PP.2~3

1 wall 2 museum 3 pilot 4 castle 5 wing 6 He is in an airplane. 7 We are in the museum. 8 Tom is in a castle. 9 ⓒ He is a pilot. 10 ⓑ She is an angel. 11 ⓐ They are spider-Man.

STORY 02 PP.4~5

1 vacation 2 feed 3 safe 4 have a meal 5 hotel 6 take a shower 7 You can take a shower with bears. 8 You can feed giraffes. 9 You can sleep with sharks. 10 ⓐ You can have a meal with sharks. 11 ⓒ You can feed lions in your room. 12 ⓑ You can take a shower with giraffes.

UNIT 02 ★ HEALTH

STORY 01 PP.6~7

1 peanut 2 dangerous 3 take medicine 4 see a doctor 5 itchy 6 He doesn't have allergies. 7 They don't take medicine. 8 James doesn't see a doctor. 9 ⓑ I don't eat shrimp. 10 ⓐ Bill doesn't eat peaches. 11 ⓒ They don't eat peanuts.

STORY 02 PP.8~9

1 taste 2 forget 3 hunger 4 gain weight 5 plate 6 exercise 7 Eat less. 8 Brush your teeth. 9 Ride a bicycle. 10 ⓒ Brush your teeth. 11 ⓐ Put the apples on a plate. 12 ⓑ Do some exercises.

UNIT 03 ★ SPECIAL JOBS

STORY 01 PP.10~11

1 miss 2 perfect 3 chance 4 lie down 5 leave 6 You can play computer games. 7 They can get money. 8 He can leave the bed. 9 ⓑ He can play games. 10 ⓐ I can watch TV. 11 ⓒ She can sleep.

STORY 02 PP.12~13

1 chew 2 swallow 3 strange 4 worried 5 pet 6 Is she happy? 7 Are you worried about my health? 8 Is he strange? 9 ⓐ Is he happy? 10 ⓒ Are you worried about the test? 11 ⓑ Am I strange?

UNIT 04 ★ HOBBIES

STORY 01 PP.14~15

1 skate 2 pass 3 fall down 4 jump 5 hurt 6 Amy runs far. 7 She goes to the bookstore. 8 I skate very well. 9 ⓒ She likes skating. 10 ⓑ He passes her quickly. 11 ⓐ She jumps very high.

STORY 02 PP.16~17

1 collect 2 famous 3 touch 4 unlock 5 locked 6 I want to collect superheroes. 7 They want to play with robots. 8 He wants to unlock the cabinet. 9 ⓒ I want to play computer games. 10 ⓑ She wants to play with dolls. 11 ⓐ He wants to have toys.

UNIT 05 ☆ NATURE

STORY 01 PP.18~19

1 hide 2 bring 3 scared 4 each other 5 protect 6 They are very scared. 7 You bring me delicious food. 8 The fish is hungry. 9 ⓑ They are scared. 10 ⓐ She can cook delicious food. 11 ⓒ We are good friends.

STORY 02 PP.20~21

1 sticky 2 weak 3 sunny 4 shine 5 set away 6 I can't eat an ant. 7 They can't see my house. 8 The butterfly can't get away. 9 ⓑ We can't move. 10 ⓐ I can't catch them.

UNIT 06 ☆ SCHOOL LIFE

STORY 01 PP.22~23

1 erase 2 sweep 3 wipe 4 trash can 5 empty 6 plant 7 It's time to clean the classroom. 8 It's time to water the plant. 9 It's time to wipe the windows. 10 ⓑ It's time to move the desks. 11 ⓐ It's time to go home. 12 ⓒ It's time to sweep the floor.

STORY 02 PP.24~25

1 wash 2 favorite 3 get up 4 get dressed 5 have breakfast 6 Do they clean the classroom? 7 Does she have a brother? 8 Does he get dressed? 9 ⓑ Do they have breakfast? 10 ⓐ Does she wash her face? 11 ⓒ Do you get up early?

UNIT 07 ☆ SAVE THE EARTH

STORY 01 PP.26~27

1 recycle 2 action 3 waste 4 bottles 5 save the Earth 6 Let's put bottles in the blue box. 7 Let's protect the Earth. 8 Let's use these things again. 9 ⓑ Let's clean the park. 10 ⓐ Let's collect cans in the box.

STORY 02 PP.28~29

1 break 2 visit 3 spend 4 polar bear 5 the North Pole 6 tour 7 Don't break the glass. 8 Don't visit the North pole. 9 Don't tour by ship. 10 ⓑ Don't visit the park. 11 ⓐ Don't catch fish here. 12 ⓒ Don't break the ice.

UNIT 08 ☆ FAIRY TALES

STORY 01 PP.30~31

1 woods 2 bread 3 cold 4 yummy 5 be lost 6 There are some cookies. 7 There is a door. 8 There are three windows. 9 ⓑ There are two houses. 10 ⓒ There is a window. 11 ⓐ There is yummy food.

STORY 02 PP.32~33

1 lamp 2 magic 3 wish 4 comic book 5 cozy 6 Here are three books. 7 Here is a yummy pizza. 8 Here are some wishes. 9 ⓒ Here is a magic lamp. 10 ⓑ Here is a cozy bed. 11 ⓐ Here are comic books.

MEMO

MEMO

MEMO

MEMO

MEMO